Praise for

Millennials & Management
and Lee Caraher

"Lee Caraher has captured what the Millennial generation demands from their employers and shows businesses how to harness the power of this new generation to co-create successful, energized businesses of the future, in which everyone will benefit, right now."
—Nilofer Merchant, Thinkers 50 #1 Future Thinker, 2013; author of *11 Rules for Creating Value in the #SocialEra*

"Millennials & Management cuts through the theory and rhetoric and gives managers and employees alike a clear way forward for successful teams and workplaces. A must-read for leaders who want to future-proof their businesses, Lee Caraher's funny, concise, and practical advice is easy to follow and will make a huge difference in your organization right away."
—Larry Weber, chairman and CEO, Racepoint Global; owner, W2 Group; author of *The Digital Marketer: Ten New Skills You Must Learn to Stay Relevant and Customer-Centric*

"Finally a book that gets beyond the survey data and the myths and provides practical advice for anyone who works with Millennials. Lee Caraher writes from personal experience in a clear, conversational style with real-life examples and a sense of humor. Must reading for anyone who supervises young employees or leads a business or non-profit in twenty-first century America. Enterprising Millennials will also find value in this book."
—John Boland, president & CEO, KQED, San Francisco

"I didn't think it possible to capture the nuances of all the complex demographic groups now roaming around the workplace. In *Millennials & Management*, Lee Caraher has done just that in a concise and compelling way. There were times when I said to myself, 'Hey, I know that person.' What Lee tells us, is how to deal with that person to create a successful organization. A must-read for all managers."

—Dr. Richard A. Moran, president of Menlo College;
author of *Navigating Tweets, Feats and Deletes*

"It's been said Millennials are unruly, unmanageable. But after reading Lee Caraher's *Millennials & Management*, I wonder how the workforce will manage without them. Boomers brought their daughters and sons to work; Millennials are bringing their dreams. And that's good for everyone. Incisive, practical, timely—from a been-there, managed-Millennials-well CEO.

—Whitney Johnson, author of *Dare, Dream, Do: Remarkable Things Happen When You Dare to Dream*

"With a mix of research, real-world stories, and easy-to-understand and implement instruction, Lee Caraher provides a refreshing, optimistic way forward that will get everyone working together and keep Boomers and Xers engaged in the workplace as Millennials become the largest generation at work."

—Keith Kitani, CEO, Guidespark employee communications and engagement

"*Millennials & Management* is a primer on how to skillfully lead this emerging segment of our work population now and into the future. Lee Caraher offers a wealth of tools and techniques to address even the thorniest management dilemmas. Both the experienced supervisor and novice to staff leadership will find immense value in her sage words."

—Mitchell Friedman, EdD, APR, Associate Dean, Student Affairs and Career Development, Presidio Graduate School

"Millennials are a pivotal part of today's working environment and defining culture. Caraher cracks the code on how to create a high-functioning intergenerational workplace built for tomorrow with a funny telling of real-world work experiences that everyone will recognize. Read it with your colleagues and help them grow, engage, and succeed today."

—Jerry Ervin, president & CEO Paragon Strategies, Management Training and Consulting

Millennials

&

Management

Millennials

&

Management

The Essential Guide to
MAKING IT WORK
at Work

Lee Caraher

bibliomotion
books + media

First published by Bibliomotion, Inc.
39 Harvard Street
Brookline, MA 02445
Tel: 617-934-2427
www.bibliomotion.com

Printed in the United States of America

Library of Congress Cataloging-in-Publication Data

Caraher, Lee.
  Millennials & management : the essential guide to making it work at work / Lee Caraher.
    pages cm
  Summary: "Millennials & Management: The Essential Guide to Making it Work at Work addresses how to motivate, collaborate with, and manage the millennial generation—who now make up almost 50% of the American workforce"—Provided by publisher.
    ISBN 978-1-62956-027-4 (hardback) — ISBN 978-1-62956-028-1 (ebook) — ISBN 978-1-62956-029-8 (enhanced ebook)
    1. Personnel management. 2. Generation Y—Employment. 3. Diversity in the workplace—Management. 4. Intergenerational relations. 5. Employee motivation. I. Title. II. Title: Millennials and management.
    HF5549.C2897 2014
    658.30084'4—dc23
                                                    2014027245

Contents

Introduction

When I started Double Forte, a public relations and digital marketing agency, in 2002 with my friend Dan Stevens (who has now moved on from the business), we were determined to have a better day, every day, than we'd had in our previous jobs. The two mandates: (1) our company would be independent and small, and (2) we'd have no twentysomethings to babysit—I had had it with the younger generation in my previous job, where I'd had hundreds of them in my group.

In 2002, these mandates were easy to realize. Large agency holding companies were still reeling from the 2000 tech bubble burst (for tech centers San Francisco, Boston, and Seattle), and wouldn't be investing or acquiring smaller companies in my neck of the woods for a while. And in San Francisco you couldn't swing a dead cat without hitting a great PR/communications person with at least ten years of experience who needed a job. Life was good, in relative terms, as we embarked on our business, and off we were to start the slow and steady process of building a business that would fund our lives.

By 2008 our model was working well, and business has grown every year, to a staff of eighteen. Some of those holding companies were interested in buying our business, but we weren't interested in changing our lives too much. And then the market changed it for us.

September 15, 2008, I started the day rearranging my workload so I could work three or four days per week, and by the end of the day, thought I'd be lucky to have a ten-hour day seven days a week to manage through the drop in the market and the consequences that would be felt by our clients, and therefore by us.

We managed pretty well through the rest of the year. But as we entered 2009, it was clear to me that we were going to have to change our model. For one thing, we were going to run out of those experienced people who liked to work soon; almost no one had been hired in our industry from late 2000 to 2004, so people with ten years of experience were going to be pretty scarce. And to ensure more flexibility in the business we needed to lower our overhead percentage, which meant hiring people at much lower salaries than those the experienced, older professionals required.

We changed our model to ensure our future, and assimilated younger, less experienced staff. Our model is different from that of most other agencies. As I described it to a dozen peers in San Francisco, New York, and Boston, I got a lot of lightbulbs of appreciation and then, "That sounds great…let me know how it goes, because I'll never be able to do that." I knew I was on to something promising, but we were going to have to figure it out without help from others who had done it before, because no one had done it before, as far as I could tell.

Hiring our first Millennial was a watershed moment. This young woman's work was fantastic. But. She brought her "service" dog, a Chihuahua-pug mix to work without asking, and thus began the parade of everyone else's newly-minted "service" dogs. She brought lots of new ideas and opportunities into my office, which I loved but didn't quite know what to do with. And she asked for four weeks off before her wedding, five weeks before the wedding. (To her credit, when her manager explained why the time off wasn't possible, the lightbulb went on.) This woman is phenomenal, and I'd hire her back in a millisecond (she moved out of the area to be closer to her family), but working with her forced me to realize that we weren't in Kansas anymore. Mostly, she made it clear that what worked for Generation X would not work for Millennials.

I looked for help from colleagues across the country to no avail—everyone was struggling with how to work with Millennials. I read everything I could get my hands on, but was put off by the "bitter Boomers" who wrote or contributed to the conversation. I was determined to have a positive attitude about figuring it out, even when the notion of adjusting drove me crazy.

After challenging ourselves to rethink our assumptions, we tweaked our model a bit to maximize the dynamics that Gen Y brought to the workplace; since then, Double Forte has been successful in closing the gap between the generations in our office.

Our business now has thirty-plus staffers, fully half—but no more than half—of whom are Millennials. We have very low turnover in a hot job market, and are lucky to have many candidates to choose from when we hire. My work, advising clients on external and internal communications, has changed dramatically in the last three years; I now spend a good chunk of time advising companies on how to work with, communicate with, and market to Millennials. I also advise on this topic to the nonprofit organizations on whose boards I sit. My phone seems to ring two or three times a month with people asking for time to talk about these struggles in their own workplaces.

In addition to drawing on my own experience with my clients and associates, I interviewed and surveyed hundreds of working people across the country in a wide range of industries and of many different ages and experience levels. I've included many of their stories in the book, and you'll recognize these personalities in your own work I'm sure. Because about half of the people asked me not to use their names, I have changed all of the names in the book of people who told them their stories and I do not name the companies. What you'll find in *Millennials & Management* is a compilation of practices that will help you make the most of your generationally diverse workforce; by reading about a wide range of experiences and ideas, you can take the best nuggets for your situation and apply them to create a cross-generational environment built for success today and tomorrow.

If you're a Boomer or Gen X leader struggling to understand the Millennials in your office, or if you're a Millennial trying to get through to your Boomer or Gen X boss, this book is for you. Understanding the perspectives of other generations and putting into practice the techniques I describe will create a smoother-running, more positive workplace for everyone.

Managers, this book will shed light on the Millennial mindset and help you find ways to work more productively with your younger colleagues, as well as appreciate the value they can bring to your business. I encourage you to read this book *with* your teams and discuss what rings true for your organizations, as well as look at how to apply the simple tenets I discuss to make your workplace work for everyone.

Millennials, read this book! You will get a good sense of why your older colleagues seem frustrated, and you will find easy-to-follow steps that will help you ease yourself onto a team or into the workplace. If you're a recent college graduate, you will find information that will make it easier for you to get hired and transition smoothly into an office.

Parents of Millennials: this book is for you, too. Within it you will find ways to help your young adult children without hurting their chances and opportunities.

We *can* all work together well, I promise! The people and companies that figure this out now will have a significant strategic advantage over those that drag their feet. Remember, no one builds a successful company or career by themselves. The need to work with other people is one of the only constants in business. If we can bridge the gap between the generations in the office, and bring our distinct strengths to the table, we will be able to co-create positive, future-proof businesses in which Boomers, Gen Xers, and Millennials can prosper together

PART 1

Millennials & Management

Today's Dynamic

1

Boomer Reality

Boomers are so bitter.
—*Ted, age twenty-eight*

I've got nothing good to say." That's the answer I got when I asked a senior executive in a large Saint Louis marketing firm to talk with me about his experience with Millennials in his workplace, where more than fifty out of the 120-person staff are between twenty-two and thirty years of age. While it's perhaps a bit extreme, this executive's attitude sums up the general feeling I've encountered from Baby Boomers (born 1946–1964) and late Gen Xers (born 1965–1979) as I explored ways to bridge the gap that seems to exist everywhere between older management and Millennials (born 1980–2000), particularly the younger of the cohort.

A quick Internet search on working with Millennials, also known as Generation Y, gives the impression that bitter feelings about the younger generation are a new phenomenon and that Baby Boomers are the first generation to deal with the "ungrateful youth" around them. Ha!

Thousands of years ago Plato wrote in Socrates' voice,[1] "The children now love luxury; they have bad manners, contempt for authority; they show disrespect for elders and love chatter in place of exercise. Children are now tyrants, not the servants of their households. They no longer rise when elders enter the room. They contradict their parents, chatter before company, gobble up dainties at the table, cross their legs, and

tyrannize their teachers." Sounds pretty current, although I'm
not sure I've ever had a "dainty."

Generational Definitions[2]

Millennials: The generation born 1980–2000
Generation X: The generation born 1965–1979
Baby Boomers: The generation born 1946–1964
Silent Generation: The generation born 1925–1945
The Greatest Generation: The generation born before
1901- 1924

The Bible is full of stories of generational discontent; the
Middle Ages progress from one contentious generation gap to
another over a period of five hundred years (finally, my degree
in medieval history is applicable!); characters in Jane Austen's
Regency novels comment on "young men these days;" and, of
course, Paul Lynde in *Bye Bye Birdie* summed it all up when he
sang, "What's the matter with kids today?" Generational divides
are nothing new: but now we're the ones who have to deal with
it, so it feels like a new, heavy, and more important dilemma.

While I generally dislike generalizations, I think many Baby
Boomers and Gen Xers have talked themselves into bitter discontent about the Millennials in their workplaces based on
(1) the reality Boomers and Xers face in their own lives and
careers and (2) a set of misappropriated myths that perpetuate
complaint. These two dynamics combine to create a negative
point of view for many Boomers and Xers as they enter the last
decade, or more likely *decades*, of their careers. And we've got
a long way to go; the vast majority of Boomers can't just retire
their way out of working with younger generations. If you're
anywhere between forty and sixty, you may have ten to thirty-
five years left in your working life. Now is the time to find a
way to work more productively with the younger cohort; to
ignore this opportunity is to consign yourself to misery.

My own plan to retire by age fifty was a pipe dream to start with, and it is nowhere near a possibility today—and not only because that birthday passed in March. Part of this change in plan is because of the way my husband and I have chosen to educate our children; part of this is having a special needs child and the unplanned costs associated with that; part of this is the reality of entrepreneurship; but most of this is because I've had to recover large losses in my conservatively invested savings four times since I started working after college, and my salary stalled at points during trying economic times over the last twenty-five years.

Boomer Story: Gail, sixty-seven

"I opened up my statement in October 2008 and found that I'd lost 40 percent of my retirement fund. Forty percent. Forty percent, two months before I was supposed to retire at sixty-two," shares Gail, a recently retired health-care administrator. Gail knew right then that she would not be able to fulfill her retirement plans, and renegotiated with her employer to stay on; she retired five years later, at sixty-seven, in September 2013.

Boomer Reality

And I am not alone—Boomer after Boomer shared with me stories of having to work longer because they have not saved enough and because they lost so much of their retirement savings in the downturn of 2008 and 2009. People are living longer and need more money than they had planned. Health care is expensive, and with our longer lives we can expect that health-related expenses will grow larger than anyone had anticipated. Housing is finally starting to catch up to pre-2007 valuation drops, but according to Zillow, at least 20 percent of all U.S. homeowners are still either underwater, recovering from foreclosure, or catching up from selling short. As Paul Taylor describes in *The Next America*, "more than 10,000 Baby Boomers are retiring every single day, most of them not as well prepared financially as they'd hoped."[3] A 2013 Gallup Survey showed that "more than a third of workers expect to retire after sixty-five, up significantly from 14 percent in 1995 ... and only a quarter of adults are hoping to retire before age sixty-five, down from 49 percent in 1995."[4] What looked sweet and possible in the prosperous 1990s is a distant and misconstrued memory.

If the full retirement age moves from sixty-seven as the age at which standard Social Security Benefits can be taken for people born in 1960 or later to seventy, as is currently under discussion in certain corners of Congress, the issue will be compounded. "Everyone is going to have to run faster and faster to stay in place at work, and that makes it more difficult for us to remain employed," explains Sara Rix, PhD, senior strategic policy advisor at AARP. And once older people leave their longtime jobs, she adds, "In this economy, it's pretty tough to find something else."

If you're a woman bringing home the bacon for your family, as more and more women are today, the fact that you will likely earn seventy-seven cents[5] to eighty-two cents[6] on the dollar, depending on the report, compared with men in the same position makes the picture a bit bleaker. Employed women will need to work even longer than men, or save a higher percentage of their income every year, to build the nest egg they will need to retire and not need financial support from their families in their later years.

The forty-nine-to-sixty age group is a really "tricky spot to be in," says Ted, forty-eight, the general manager of a large international enterprise software company. "You can see people get pushed to the sidelines. They've reached their peak or slowed down, and it can be both demotivating and scary to everyone around them. They're constantly on the watch to being replaced or displaced."

Boomer Story: Chris, age fifty-four

"I have two sets of friends. The smaller group who has made it on Wall Street or in real estate and been lucky with their timing have retired early and are enjoying life—they're all good. But the much larger group of my peers and friends don't have near enough to retire, see that the world is changing, and realize that they need to hang on until retirement, because if they have to change jobs, they might not get one, since the jobs we're qualified for are going to smart, younger, less expensive folks."

One Millennial posted in the comments section of an online story about why Millennials are unhappy: "Now hurry the hell up and retire...it's time to make some god damn room for a...generation that's clambering to find a decent entry level job but can't because you're holding all the cards."[7]

In response, a late Baby Boomer put this issue in perspective by posting back, "A lot of us STILL haven't gotten where we were heading. Regardless of our education level, if we didn't have powerful family connections, we had to work at McJobs and build our resumes on volunteer work before we got our first 'real' jobs that had anything to do with the degrees we earned. Many of us are still not where we wanted to be, and we're pushing retirement age, so we can't just step aside."

Personally, I'm anticipating needing to work at least another fifteen years to earn what my family needs for retirement, and so are so many millions of fifty-year-olds across the country. That means I need to be productive and consistently relevant in the workplace for a long time to come. I believe nothing will keep me more relevant than being recognized for understanding Millennials and optimizing my working relationship with them.

What About Generation X?

With most Boomers anticipating longer working futures and Millennials growing in sheer numbers and percentages in the office, the squeeze is on for Generation X. The smallest cohort in the workplace, Xers find themselves in the tough position of waiting for Boomers to exit and/or in the hugely opportunistic position of creating a bridge between the two generations on either side of them.

For the GenX man ready to step into Gail's position when she first anticipated her retirement in 2008 before she lost 40 percent of her retirement fund, and for many others like him, advancement was delayed for more than five years. And with the delay came less compensation, less opportunity, and less security for millions of GenXers waiting to fulfill their careers.

In 2012, Dimensional Research, a provider of technology market research, found that "Gen X is the most demanding age group" in the global workplace. Gen X employees are more likely than either Millennials or Baby Boomers to ask for higher job titles, promotions, off-cycle bonuses or salary increases, flexible hours, reduced hours, and flexible work locations.[8]

Delayed salary increases or job interruptions due to the Great Recession coupled with financial responsibilities such as children and aging parents are definitely creating a squeeze for Gen X. "We've all waited to be able to get what the Baby Boomers had and now the Millennials are demanding benefits and salaries that we had to wait for," wrote an anonymous Gen X woman in my survey. "No wonder Millennials are driving us crazy."

The opportunity for Generation X is to become an effective bridge between Boomers and Millennials. The first step is to understand the dynamics on both sides of the bookends, and to grasp and master the mind-set of Millennials, who are products of a different environment, culture, education, and upbringing.

2

Kids These Days

You can't argue that they have great qualities, and that
they have lots to offer, even if they drive you crazy.
— *Ciara, age forty-eight*

According to Pew Research,[1] there are more than seventy-seven million Millennials, born since 1980, who in 2014 are between twenty-two and thirty-four years of age. This generation eclipses Generation X's forty-six million by almost 68 percent, and generally equals the size of the Baby Boomer generation which the U.S. Census Bureau counts at 76.4 million (Population Reference Bureau).

It's important to remember that Millennials are not all alike. Derek Thompson, senior editor at the *Atlantic,* notes that the Millennials born between 1980 and 1986 "landed in the cradle during an awful recession, learned to walk during the Reagan recovery, came of age in the booming 1990s, and entered the labor market after the Sept. 11 attacks and before the Great Recession, the two tragedies of the early 21st century."[2] Millennials born between 1986 and 1992 have entered—or tried to enter—the job market during or at the tail end of the Great Recession. Those born since 1992 are now in school and facing a decidedly different reality than those born at the beginning of the generation. And the huge size of the cohort tells you that we can expect Millennials to have the same type of dynamic and sweeping impact on American culture that the Baby Boomers have had in the last twenty years (and will continue to have, in a different way, as they age).

What the size doesn't tell you is the key differences between this generation and those that came before it.

> ## Millennial Insight: Liz, age thirty
>
> "I've heard all the negative stuff about Millennials—that we're lazy, want life–work balance more than is reasonable, use technology too much—and I really don't identify with that. But then I took the Pew Millennial test and I scored a 96, so I guess there's more to it than the bad stuff."

Since 2008, a set of bitter myths about Millennials have emerged and been perpetuated to the point that they have taken on a life of their own. I count six prevalent myths:

Myth #1: Millennials are entitled.
Myth #2: Millennials expect rewards and promotions just for showing up.
Myth #3: Millennials don't work hard.
Myth #4: Millennials can't get anything done and don't take initiative.
Myth #5: Millennials are casual and disrespectful.
Myth #6: Millennials aren't willing to pay their dues, and want freedom, flexibility, and work–life balance from the outset.

Most of these myths are false, a couple are plausible, and one is true. Behind each myth is a gap in understanding that we must bridge in order to deal with management's frustration and start harnessing the incredible talent Millennials bring to the party. For Millennials, understanding why their older colleagues are frustrated is the first step they can take to help make the workplace better...for everyone. Before we explore these myths, it's important to review a few differences in the way Millennials see the world compared with Boomers and Gen-Xers.

My Own Experience: A Tale of Two Millennials

In a moment of particular weakness in 2011, I hit the speakerphone on the table where I was giving an informational interview to the daughter of a former colleague, and dialed him. The woman had just declared that her dad had "told me you have a job for me." I apologized to my former colleague, the young woman's father, if there was a misunderstanding, but no, I did not "have a job for" his daughter. Silence ensued, and I could hear the father swear under his breath before he said, "No, Lee, I'm sorry. I was very clear that you said you had no open positions." (I knew this because he had confirmed that fact in an e-mail prior to the interview.)

The daughter was nonplussed. After we hung up the phone, she told me that she'd had an offer from another well-respected firm, but that she had "turned them down because it didn't pay enough" to allow her to live by herself in one of the most exclusive parts of San Francisco. "I need to make at least double what they offered," she explained.

After confirming that the offered salary (mid-forties) was very good for an entry-level job, I told her that she was "terribly misinformed" if she thought she'd get paid $90,000 at this stage in her career. She left in a huff. I called her father back and confessed to him what I'd told her, and found that I'd been the one to inform him that she'd had an offer from a good company. By the time she got home, her father and mother had defined a new set of rules for their daughter.

The following day, I was so impressed with another informational interviewer that I offered the young woman a paid internship I didn't have. Of course, her story was diametrically opposed to the first.

Catherine had realized that her chosen artistic career path would quickly dead-end in salary potential and that she could pursue her passion by volunteering or moonlighting in community theater while pursuing a more lucrative career. She moved home after fulfilling her commitments at her original dream job in a high-profile repertory company's art department, got a job at the Apple Store in her town, paid her mom rent, and started blogging so she could demonstrate her writing skills.

Over the course of an hour, she impressed me with her intellect, her focus, her initiative, her strong belief in herself, her humility, and her desire to learn. She got an internship we didn't have, much to the consternation of my CFO, and then we hired her as a full-time employee after three months; she stayed with us for three years before she moved to Austin for family reasons.

Digitally Native

Millennials are the first digitally native generation, growing up with technology touching virtually every aspect of their lives. Frankly, gadgets seem to grow from their extremities—Darwin would have had a field day.

Gen Yers have grown from toddlers to college graduates with seemingly endless sources of technology-enabled distraction, real or perceived. Over the past fifteen years, teachers have struggled to find the right balance between using computer, tablet, or phone screens effectively in the classroom and teaching in a more traditional style. The commoditization of chips, screens, and other technologies has resulted in homes full of computer-aided gadgets, digital services, and technology that operate simultaneously and at increasingly fast speeds. All of this has tremendous impact on the workplace.

Time-Shifting, Second Screens, and TV without TVs

Brought up with five hundred channels of television programming of dubious quality or cultural value, Millennials now watch less and less live television. Instead, they increasingly prefer to time-shift their favorite shows using DVRs or streaming what they want, when they want, where they want onto their computers, tablets, or phones. Also, for this generation, and increasingly for Gen Xers and Baby Boomers alike, simply watching doesn't deliver the engaging experience they crave— more than 70 percent of people with tablets or smartphones are simultaneously watching television while viewing and interacting with companion information on their second screens.[3]

Media's ability to provide instant gratification is just one piece of the "want it now" sentiment so many managers complain about when talking of their Millennial team members. One Baby Boomer senior leader from Chicago observes that Millennials "like variety and a fast pace, and seem to be very confident in multitasking. I've walked into some offices full of people where you could hear a pin drop because no one was talking, yet everyone had their headphones on and was working on two large screens plus had their mobile phones and tablets in their hands." This phenomenon has two large impacts in the office environment. First, "live" doesn't carry the same weight with Millennials that it does with older generations, except in sports programming. This translates into a "don't need to be here now" attitude and the general understanding that "my time" is more important than the "show's" time. In an on-demand world, Millennials have grown up getting the media and entertainment they want, when they want it, increasingly on any device they want it on. The concept of time and place is different for Millennials than it is for those of older generations, who grew up waiting for the next episode to play on Tuesday at 9 p.m. It is a different mind-set.

Digital Communicators

Millennials, and increasingly Gen Xers and Boomers, are dependent on their mobile devices and computers to communicate. The difference between the generations here is that Millennials overwhelmingly prefer e-mail, texting, and chatting on social messaging platforms to phone conversations or even face-to-face conversations. How often have you seen a group of twentysomethings sitting at a restaurant together, all swiping and typing on their phones instead of actually talking with one another?

"What hits me right between the eyes is the difference in communication styles between me and the Millennials I work with in my company and at our client's," says Susan, a forty-seven-year-old senior executive in a Minneapolis-based sales distribution company. "Millennials are very dependent on [short-form digital] communication. They don't know their landline numbers; they don't even set up their landline voice-mail boxes at work. Everything is on e-mail or text...I never thought I'd have a sales relationship with my customer over text messaging."

Of course, Millennials don't seem able to make decisions by e-mail, text, or IM, unlike their older colleagues. Sometimes, on bad days, I want to have a cannon shoot glitter confetti every time I get a definitive answer on e-mail. "The only way we can actually get to a decision is to have an in-person meeting," continues Susan, "I'll be talking, and they'll be looking at their screens and nodding their heads a lot, but at least I'll get a definite answer because they can't go anywhere."

Every manager I talked with commented that decision making is happening in person, while time is eaten up with written communication that often lacks clarity on the writing end and comprehension on the reading end. Digital communication is dependent on words, acronyms, and emoticons, but this has not led to more effective written communication. On the contrary, while words are key to good business communication, effective writing that delivers nuance and impact and understanding is difficult to find in the workplace, no matter the age of the employee.

Access to Anything and Anyone

The world is flat to Millennials, who are used to having access to virtually any information they want, when they want it. With nearly unfettered access to billions of pages of information from around the world through the Internet, Gen Y is used to getting their hands on any data point they seek. As Millennials move into the workforce, they expect the transparency they perceive in their lives to be equally present in the office. "Transparency is key—information is readily available. We are very educated and we can see what else is out there," explains Andrew, twenty-seven, an associate at a real estate investment firm in New York City. Whether that data is accurate or not, or whether it is well supported, is a different conversation.

With easy access to so much, Millennials also seem much more worldly than their older colleagues. "I'm really impressed with the sophistication and breadth of experiences of the Millennials I see," says Ted, the forty-eight-year old manager. "They've travelled, they've tried lots and lots of different foods, they know a lot about the world. They have very sophisticated tastes compared to my peers when I was their age." Andrew adds, "Our generation grew up with access to the world, and I feel like we want to see and experience more of it than other generations."

Just as access to any information is taken for granted, so is access to anybody. This is the first generation that has been raised to call their parents' friends and their friends' parents by their first names. Millennials are used to being one e-mail or click away from communicating directly with companies and their leaders. Introductory e-mails that start with "Hey, Lee, good to meet you," from unknown young people seeking an interview for an entry-level job, are common in my inbox.

While this informality may be welcome in social situations,

in the workplace it can immediately break down any sense of hierarchy, and for some older people, lessen the sense of respect they expect or feel is appropriate.

More Educated, but Different

While the media likes to celebrate the wild success of college dropouts Mark Zuckerberg and his predecessors Bill Gates, Steve Jobs, and Michael Dell, this generation is our most educated.[4] Workers with a college degree are driving a greater disparity in earning potential. According to the Pew Research Center, a college education is worth more today, as "there's a wider earnings gap between college-educated and less-educated Millennials compared with all previous generations."[5]

At the same time, the quality of education has changed significantly; greater emphasis on measuring teacher effectiveness has led to a generation raised to ace the test rather than master the material. It seems like they "know a little about everything and in a lot of cases not a lot about anything—perhaps depth of knowledge is not as important to them?" asks Margaret, fifty-one, who works with a large team, half of whom are under thirty.

Despite the good educations so many Gen Yers have, compared with their predecessors, Gen Y frequently gets dinged for seeking an easy way out. "They think there's an easy digital answer to everything, and don't understand that there are ways to know things without just clicking on something," suggests Matt, an early Gen Xer at forty-seven. "They don't seem to care about what's behind the click, and don't seem to know that the first thing they see on a search result is not the only or best answer—it's just about getting things done fast."

In the workplace this shows up in two ways: the ability to get started and the ability to finish. I work with a lot of Millennials who "are pretty frickin' bright," says Jeff, a marketing associate at a large, established online media company in New York, "but I don't see that they work any better" than people from other generations. "Instead, I see they are not as good at self-motivating and definitely aren't as accountable for their work." Ted stresses that Millennials need "more context, more explanation, and more direction" to get started on a project. And they need a lot more guidance and feedback to get anything done.

Gen X Insight: Ted, age forty-five

"I don't think my younger colleagues have an appreciation for mastering a skill. What strikes me about them is that they aren't going to let perfection be the enemy of progress, and getting things off their plates is the priority at the expense of quality."

Peter, forty-five, a social worker, adds, "This [difficulty completing tasks] manifests itself in tasks that are 70 percent done and things aren't wrapped up as you'd expect them to be. When I go back to my people to get the work finished, I don't get a lot of pushback, but the follow-up is not that much better. So I either have to finish it myself or find someone else more senior to get it done."

The partial-work phenomenon was a constant theme in interviews with Baby Boomer and Gen X managers, who consistently complain, "They just can't seem to get to the end of things—they just don't know how to cross the finish line." In my own work, I found that these two dynamics were flourishing until we laid out a different path to collaboration and success, which I discuss in chapter 4.

I think that part of this widespread issue is due to the rampant grade inflation that permeates secondary schools, colleges, and universities nationwide. A lot has been written about this trend, which Stuart Rojstaczer and Christopher Healy wrote extensively about in *The Teachers College Record* in 2010. *The Washington Post* reported on a mistakenly sent e-mail that revealed that almost everyone at the University of Virginia Law School was above average. One PhD candidate revealed in an article that "the real reason so many of us inflate grades is to avoid students complaining."

Many Millennials have been educated in a system where negotiation is part of the modus operandi, and when they enter the workplace they simply don't know how to cope with feedback that is not negotiable. Who to complain to when they have to re-do the work? Why isn't this good enough? How did I become average when I graduated with honors?

We could talk a lot about this, and what a disservice grade inflation is to these students. While business probably has little impact in fixing the problem, businesses big and small have to clean up the mess that grade inflation creates in the workplace.

Parents Still Matter

Importantly, many Millennials have been raised by Xers and Boomers who have intervened at almost every difficult step along the way, consistently validating their children's existence with awards and trophies for participation, not necessarily excellence, encouraging them to "not settle" and building a self-confidence based on input instead of achievement. "My mom is really close to being my best friend," says Carolyn, twenty-five, in a comment I heard over and over again. "I can count on her to help me with anything."

This generation has been raised with more two-income families, in which the parents have had to plan every moment of the day, observes Ciara. "The Millennials I know at work and in my family have never had 'free play.' They've had organized play since they were toddlers, and their parents resolved all their conflicts for them, either because they were trying to help or because they didn't have time for their kids to take up their time to work it out."

John, fifty-four, a senior sales executive, gets right to the point, "Our generation has to be the worst parents ever!

Millennial Insight: Chris, age twenty-six

"As a so-called Millennial, the problem I see among many of my peers is that, unlike previous generations, we've grown up being told we can do anything we want to do, be anyone we want to be. We've been wrapped up in cotton wool, so to speak, by overprotective parents, not forced to fight our own battles, and had our egos slowly and routinely stroked by parents and teachers our whole lives... largely, this is what I see.

"The friction comes when Millennials must hang up the comforts of home and academia and enter the real work world, where if you make big mistakes you get fired, and no one praises you simply for showing up. Business, or conventional business, can certainly do a better job in helping young workers adjust to being contributing members of the workforce as well as loosening up their own rigid systems—this is why I've chosen to work for a start-up rather than an established company (I feel it's stupid to have a dress code, among many other commonly accepted corporate guidelines).

"Similarly, people in my generation need to realize that success takes time, and that failure is almost an inevitable step on the road to success. In order to be a leader or be respected or praised you have to work hard and be exceptional. You don't get kudos just for making it in on time.

"I feel at times there is an entitlement in our generation—we grew up with everything exactly when we wanted it, and now that we have to wait we're too impatient. I understand the headaches that come with hiring and working with Millennials but I think there needs to be some give and take from employers as well as from us as employees."[6]

We haven't prepared them for real life, and when these kids get into the workplace and find out they don't get awards for showing up, it gets ugly." That hits close to home for me as a mother of sixteen-year-old and thirteen-year-old young men.

On my refrigerator is a list of things from *150 Ways to Show Kids You Care*[7] that's been there for at least eight years. It reads, a bit out of order from the book, like this:

- Acknowledge them.
- Ask them about themselves.
- Tell them how terrific they are.
- Listen to them.
- Say yes a lot.
- Tell them their feelings are okay.
- Suggest options when they seek your advice.
- Answer their questions.
- Make yourself available.
- Display their artwork at home.
- Thank them.
- Give them lots of compliments.

I believe in this list: I love this book, and I give it to everyone I know when they have children. However, what's not on my list are the other things that set boundaries, correct inappropriate behavior, enforce consequences consistently, and "graduate" kids through age-appropriate responsibilities. I'll throw myself into the parent group that missed that chapter on how to wean kids off of trophies for participation. By themselves, these characteristics aren't that compelling, but when combined they create a very different composite persona with whom Boomers and Gen Xers must learn to work.

Parent Trap

The irony is that the Boomers and Gen Xers complaining loudest about Millennials miss the connection between their own parenting skills and their young colleagues in the workplace. While some parents of young adults still seem to exclude their own progeny from their disappointment and frustration with their children's peers, others are staring the reality of their parenting style in the face as their kids boomerang home after college.

I have always granted any informational interview requested of me, by the interviewee or their parent or mentor. I got my first job through the generosity of informational interviews brokered by my father's best friend, and feel that it's the right thing to do. Besides generating good karma, I get a handle on what's going on outside of my organization—I highly recommend it. With these interviews comes a window into parents who have their kids at home after college graduation. I find parents of adult children split into two groups: encouragers and enablers.

The encouragers work with their grown children to define a productive path, providing a safety cushion even as they explain that no job is perfect and that learning how and when to compromise is a necessary skill. They have their kids contribute at home, either in rent or chores or both. And they maintain their rules and standards in their households regardless of how old their kids are.

"I lived at home for fourteen months after college, and, yes, I did count," said Michelle, now twenty-seven. Michelle's parents didn't have her pay rent, but did tell her she needed to "grin and bear it" when she got work that she didn't like. "They wanted me to be happy and supported me changing jobs," but insisted that she not leave one job before she had another one.

The enablers, on the other hand, don't require much of their kids, which often leads to backlash from other Millennials and employers alike. "I don't understand these helicopter parents who are working for their kids," says Georgia, twenty-seven from Philadelphia. "It's crazy what these Boomer parents are doing, and it's crazy for these twentysomethings to let them—it's not helping them." Liz, thirty, adds that she doesn't have a lot of respect for her peers who count on their parents to make their way: "I don't have mommy or daddy paying for my rent or car like so many of the Millennials I know do...it's going to come back to haunt them. It already does haunt them in the office." These employees are pegged as slackers and therefore get sidelined for career-advancing assignments.

And Millennials are bringing their parents into the workplace like never before. Karie Willyerd, VP of learning and social adoption at SuccessFactors, a large HR solutions provider, believes that parents may very well be (the) "secret weapon in convincing Millennials to join or stay" at an organization.[8] Stories of parents getting involved in their grown children's careers abound. Willyerd notes that between one-third and one-half of the hundreds of HR executives she speaks with every year have firsthand experience of parents interfering with hiring or performance reviews.

Millennials in the workplace cite their parents as more influential than any other input.[9] Of course, given that, according to Pew Research, 36 percent of Millennials age eighteen to twenty-four are still living at home, parental involvement in their careers should not be wholly unexpected.

Carol, who lives with her husband and two children under age ten while running a successful sales organization for a large national retailer, shares what her friends have told her: "So many of my friends with twentysomething kids say, 'Holy crap, we should have done things differently' and tell me that I 'still have time to not make the same mistakes' that they did."

While we could talk about the reasons behind this common parenthood philosophy for hours while prone on a therapist's couch paying $200-plus per hour, here's where we are: upbringing matters.

Boomer Story: "We Screwed Up"

Isabelle, an early Gen X senior executive shared the story of giving an internship to the daughter of one of her company's longtime business partners, a late Boomer. Isabelle said:

"Her father called us up and said 'I need a favor. My daughter's been home from college for a few months and we just realized that she doesn't know shit. We've really screwed up and she won't listen to us about what it's going to be like in the workplace. Can you help us out—don't coddle her, show her what work is like.'

"We put her to work doing intern work, and one week into it she came to me and said, 'I don't like it.' I told her, 'I don't really care if you like it or not. You need to know that this is what a first job feels like. And if you think that you're going to get dressed up and go into a senior customer meeting the second week on the job, it's not going to happen.'

"A week later she came and told us she'd taken another job overseas. Ten days into that job she e-mailed me that she'd made a mistake, saying she 'didn't know it was going to be this way,' and that her mother was on her way to bring her home.

"Then she went into a management-training program at a national retailer. She lasted three months and then e-mailed me: 'I'm looking for a new job.' Finally, she got a job at a marketing agency starting at the bottom, and she's still there two years later. Her father said she realized that she needed to buckle down, that she is twenty-six with a four-page resume and was losing her ability to find any work. And this is a kid who is super smart—what about those kids who don't have as much going for them?"

So What Now?

"We need to figure this out," says Margaret, fifty-four, a C-level executive at a large events-management company. "At my last company, we had a long string of dazzling, talented Millennials. They would consistently last six or seven months and then leave us. We could never get any of the good ones to stay—that's no way to run a business for the future."

If Millennials were far and few between, that would be one thing. However, Millennials make up a substantial portion of today's companies, and by 2020 will make up almost half, 46 percent, of the workforce.[10]

Unless your company is going to cease to exist when you decide to retire, you need to find a way to make it work at work with this growing segment of the labor force. As a bottom line, getting along and maximizing the strengths of different people in the workplace is not just a "nice to have." Those companies that learn to adapt and become places where Millennials are welcomed and appreciated *without* compromising performance standards will have a significant strategic advantage over their competition.

As Susan said, "Sometimes we look at these college graduates that we're interviewing as if exotic animals have entered our midst." For better or for worse, the workplace is not the Serengeti, and we need to understand how to work with Millennials and not just gather war stories about our encounters with them.

3

The Millennial Mind-Set

Millennials don't all come from the same mold.
We're all different; we all have different styles to achieve
greatness!

—*Petra, age twenty-six*

Millennials were raised in an entirely different ecosystem than their parents and grandparents. Not just surrounded by, but assisted by technology and all of the advances and advantages (or disadvantages depending on your point of view) that technology brought to entertainment, education, and communication, Millennials share many traits and characteristics their older colleagues do not understand or appreciate.

Of course Gen Y interprets the characteristics a bit differently. Not surprisingly, in more than one hundred interviews and surveys with people age twenty-two to thirty around the country, I found that Millennials object to the bad rap their generation gets.

"I see evidence of what people are talking about with some people my age, but I don't think it's fair that a few bad examples are making us all look bad," said Erin, twenty-four. "And I can give you lots of examples of slacker Gen Xers and Boomers in my office, and no one is saying those generations suck." Liz, thirty, adds, "A bad work ethic is a bad work ethic, not a generational thing."

Let's put this into perspective. While in the last few years, article after article has derided all Millennials as entitled and needy, it's been challenging for most college graduates to get jobs. So while this huge generation pumps out more and more debt-ridden college-educated adults eager to start their lives, the economy hasn't been able to suck them up fast enough.

In addition, many Boomers and Xers have either stalled in their careers with little upward movement in the last six years or have extended their careers to earn enough to retire on, further narrowing opportunity for younger people to advance or new people to enter the workforce. Also, since 2008, a huge cohort of Boomers and late Xers who lost their jobs in the Great Recession have not been able to find comparable new jobs, and have effectively been displaced to involuntary retirement, significantly reduced employment and/or replaced by younger, cheaper labor.

So we have a bit of a catch-22: Millennials who have been raised or influenced by peers to believe in themselves and their ability to do anything have entered, or tried to enter, the job market just as the economy had no place to put them. At the same time, economic conditions required older workers to reset their expectations. No wonder Millennials are collectively labeled "entitled"—frankly, it's a little too convenient.

How Millennials See Themselves

In contrast to how Millennials have been portrayed by countless articles, blog posts, comments, YouTube videos and even Saturday Night Live skits, Millennials have a vastly different point of view about themselves and their generation.

Millennial Mind-Set

Capable

Throughout all of the interviews, e-mails, tweets, posts, updates, and blog comments, what comes through loud and clear is how capable members of this generation believe they are. "I don't think my generation believed so much in our ability as this one does," says Abby, forty-eight, commenting on the Gen Y members of her team. (Of course, we don't know what early Boomers and their predecessors thought of us, but I'd guess the same thing!)

"I can get a lot more done than the older people in my office can," says Michelle. "I may be the youngest one in the office, but I'm the most productive one." Summing up the disconnect, Liam, twenty-six, comments, "Management underestimates my ability because of my lack of experience all the time."

One Boomer's Point of View:
Chris, age fifty-four

In talking about the high-performing Millennials who make up more than half of his fifty-person sales and marketing team, Chris says, "I think the Millennials I know work hard and get a tremendous amount of work done. They are succeeding as fast as the work lets them—it's impressive."

Sally, a longtime recruiter, describes a great generational gap between Millennials and the earlier Gen Xers and Boomers: "Every younger candidate I've ever talked with in the last five years thinks they are full of potential, and have so much to contribute right now. It's not a question of whether or not they are right for the job, it's a question of is the job right for them. This is so different from where the Gen Xers and Boomers were when they were at this age."

Contributors

Importantly, and sometimes frustratingly for their managers, Millennials want to contribute to the "real" work from day one, and do not relish the idea of working their way up the ladder, a process Boomers and Gen Xers considered the norm. "I am here to make a difference," says Michelle. "If I see a way to make something better, I will."

When her candidates are dissatisfied at jobs, explains Leslie, thirty-two, a recruiter who places many Millennials in positions across the country, "It's because they feel like they are caged in a confining box with no opportunity to do anything different." In fact, many Millennials prefer going to smaller companies where they will be able to have a bigger impact and a hands-on role. "I chose to work at a smaller company so that I can wear a lot more hats, and get a lot more exposure to different functions and jobs," says Katherine, twenty-five. "It helps me hone different skills."

This desire for important work is a key driver for Millennials, who have been pegged as job-hoppers. While 91 percent of Millennials expect to stay in their jobs for less than three years,[1] younger employees, like their older counterparts, stay longer when they understand how they fit in and how their work contributes. "I always want to feel that what I'm doing in my work is important," says Lisa, twenty-seven, who has changed jobs three times in four years. When I asked her to explain why she had moved so many times, she described positions that "looked good from the outside" but were full of menial work. "No one told me why what I was doing mattered," so she kept searching until she found a position where she felt like her work mattered.

Change Makers

Beyond feeling capable and wanting to contribute, most of the working Millennials I surveyed feel emboldened and empowered to change the world, or at least their corner of it.

Twentysomething after twentysomething expressed a strong desire to change the way business works. "I think that Millennials are more entrepreneurial and are pushing the envelope in changing business," says Abby, twenty-six. "We're helping to mold and change how business is done for the better." Abby's sentiment was echoed over and over again by her peers across the country.

Many, many Gen Yers talked about their desire to change the world for the better through their work and/or their employer's dedication to volunteerism and community service. Today, a company's allowances for volunteerism and dedicated workdays for team volunteer efforts factor importantly in many Millennials' decisions to apply to or accept positions. "I want to help effect change in my community," says Madison. "I'm so excited about my new job, because I am part of the change that is happening in the office and in the community. It's one of the reasons why I wanted to work here."

A 2012 talent report reveals that "employees who say they have the opportunity to make a direct social and environmental impact through their job reported higher satisfaction levels than those who don't."[2] When college students were queried on whether or not they'd be willing to take a 15 percent pay cut, 35 percent said they would if it meant working for a company committed to CSR (corporate social responsibility), 45 percent said yes, "for a job that makes a social or environmental impact," and 58 percent said yes, if they could work for an "organization with values like my own." Of course, most of these students are not in the job market and probably haven't started paying rent yet, however it's important to understand these factors as college graduates apply for work in our organizations.

Confident

What is crystal clear from all my discussions with older leaders and managers, Millennial workers, Millennial managers and leaders, and even Millennials who have yet to find work is that this generation is confident. They are confident that they can contribute. They are confident in their ability to learn. They are confident that they can make a difference at work and in the world around them *now*. They are confident that they matter. And they are confident that they can be fulfilled in their work as part of a meaningful life.

Along with this confidence comes a set of expectations and norms they feel are reasonable. Why? Some have learned from their parents—perhaps by how they were raised, with high level of parent involvement in their achievement, or perhaps in reaction to their parents' careers. Others have learned it from their peers at college, the great petri dish for young people evolving from hormonal teenagers into adults.

In the end, it doesn't really matter why. What matters is that we understand what our younger colleagues in the office want so that we can not only harness the energy, brain power, and technology-enabled know-how they bring to the table, but also set a new normal for work rules from which everyone— *everyone*—can benefit.

I'm not suggesting that we need to give the younger contingent everything they want. Catering to is not caving if it works for everyone and improves the outcome. However, we can adjust the way we approach the work environment, opportunity development, and work processes to help ensure a more forward-looking, future-proof workplace. To do this, we need to stop letting the pervasive myths about Millennials get in our way of seeing potential for productive change.

What Millennials Want

All people want to be happy in their work. "I am in charge of my own happiness," sums up Liz. "And a big part of that is being happy in my work." Emily, twenty-four, articulates the sentiment in a nutshell: "I'm going to be spending more time at work than on any other activity, and so if I'm going to have a happy life, I need to have a happy workday."

Don't we all!

Millennial Insight: Emily, age twenty-five

"My parents have sacrificed a lot to give me what I have— my education, my opportunities, my things. They look at work as a means to an end. I don't think they've ever really been happy in their jobs. I don't want that for myself, and I think they'd be happiest if I was happy in my work."

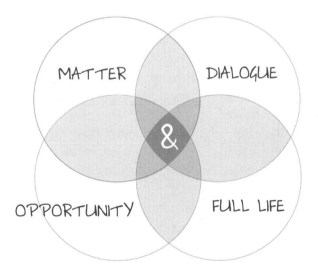

Millennials Want to Matter

Millennials want to matter in the workplace: they want their work to matter, their opinions to matter, their presence to make a meaningful difference, and they want to be part of an "awesome" team.

They want meaningful work. "It's important to me and my friends that we're doing something important for the company," says Charles, twenty-four, an assistant product manager in Chicago, echoing a strong notion that was repeated consistently by Millennials I talked with in different jobs and different industries across the country. While Baby Boomers and Gen Xers may have just done the work assigned to them early in their careers without question, do not expect Millennials to fall in line this way. " 'Because I said to' doesn't work for me," says Liz. "I need to understand how the work I'm doing matters."

They want to be heard. Participating and not just biding time until their point of view and ideas are welcome later in their careers is key for this generation. Unlike their older colleagues, who may have expected to hold their tongues and do what was asked of them, Millennials not only want to be heard but expect that their ideas will be taken seriously. "I would make suggestions about how to streamline the work and I was told that I wasn't allowed to give input on how the work would happen—I had to get out of there," says David, twenty-six.

Twenty-seven-year-old Jeff, the New York-based marketing associate, enjoys his current position in part because he's invited to comment and suggest alternatives. "My manager and her manager always ask for my opinion. My suggestions may not always be taken, but they explain why—I feel like my ideas make a difference, which is cool."

They want to be part of a great team. While Millennials often get pegged for being a "Me" generation, I found that being part of a great team ranked quite high on their priority scale. "Being part of a team with great camaraderie is much more important to me than just the work," says Grace, twenty-seven, a marketing manager at a large national apparel retailer. First, it makes the day better, but more importantly, it "could pay off later if people leave and are looking for people at their new job."

Being part of a good team is "super important," explains Amy, twenty-five, who did considerable due diligence on the team she'd be working with before accepting any interviews in her last job search. "I learned after two jobs that I needed to interview with the team I'm going to work with, so I could get a sense of the group and if it would be a good fit," she says. "The people around me are really important—if I'm not happy with the people around me, I'm not going to be happy at work."

Millennials Want Constant Dialogue

Perhaps because they've had so much digital communication and interaction and parental guidance (or interference, depending on your point of view) in their lives, Millennials expect, and seem to require, constant dialogue about their work. There is a way to channel the chatter!

They want appreciation and acknowledgement. Nothing is worse than not being noticed. It's important that senior leadership "acknowledge what we're doing here matters to them," articulates Gabe. Carla, twenty-six, acknowledges that the "trophy syndrome" for showing up is an issue, and posits that we need to find a happy medium. "A generational problem for my generation is that everyone has to win. It's a given that everyone wins. But someone has to be first, which is a hard thing to get used to" in the workplace. At the same time, "just because someone is first doesn't mean that the rest of the team doesn't matter too."

They want feedback. Millennials expect, and indeed crave, constant constructive (read positive) feedback loops. I have pages and pages of comments from the Gen Yers I talked with about the quality and the frequency of feedback—or the lack thereof—about their work and roles.

"I think I have reasonable expectations of a boss," says Liz. She believes a manager is there to "help and guide," "listen to and hear," and "to give feedback." "Unfortunately, lots of managers don't know how to, or don't bother to, give feedback," says Liz.

When talking about why she left a seemingly plum position, Julia placed a large weight on the lack of feedback she got from her managers. "I never got feedback on what I could improve, even though I asked for it. And then in my review more than a year into the job, I was told that I didn't have a good enough poker face and that I wasn't concise enough in e-mails. What? They couldn't tell me this beforehand so I could work on it?"

(For anyone thinking, "But they can't hear constructive criticism," more on that later in chapter 9.)

They want transparency. Senior managers sometimes act "like we can't find things out about the company without them," says Drew, twenty-six. "If they want to earn our respect, management needs to tell us what's going on before we find out from people outside the company or from the media."

Millennials Want a Full-Life Approach to Work

Millennials were raised in the 90s and 2000s when the quest for work–life balance dominated career discussion. They watched and listened to their working parent or parents struggle to succeed at work and at home, and most likely make sacrifices in both to accommodate both roles. They've seen what can be achieved and don't believe they need to wait to simultaneously have both a full career and full life.

They want freedom. Two distinct groups emerged in my research. The first group, what I call the Digital Freedom Crusaders, doesn't place much value on being in the office at specific times. "You don't need to know where I am as long as I'm doing the work," says Andrea, twenty-eight. "I am more productive at home, and I should be able to work from Starbucks if I want to as long as I'm getting my work done well." This group seems almost "bitter about having to be in the office," says Susan the early Gen X senior executive in Minneapolis, all of whose customers/clients are under thirty-four.

I call the other group the Office Traditionalists, and they value office hours and being together, and believe that being seen matters for advancement and participation. "I like to be in the office. I have a better thumb on the pulse of what is going on, and I've been able to jump on opportunities because I'm there when they come up," explains Mary, twenty-five.

Katherine, twenty-eight, adds, "My old company, a big accounting firm, had lots of flexibility initiatives—but there's only so much you can do in a system with so many people before it broke down."

They want work–life balance. The cry for work–life balance that has emerged in the last twenty years, first from working mothers and now from a growing contingent of working fathers, has had a big impact on the children of the people who started the conversation. "I want to enjoy my life more than my parents did or still do, and I think I should be able to now and not wait for retirement to really live my life," says Sarah, twenty-four.

Across the board, older managers and senior leaders noted that Millennials are demanding work–life balance from the beginning of their careers. "Another thing I find interesting in a refreshing way is that Millennials are less willing to compromise on work–life tradeoffs than my peers did or do," comments Ted. "They don't want to commute far, their workplace fits what they like to do—bike, walk, eat, be close to other activities—and they are willing to trade off for these work–life fit factors over jobs that don't have them." Carol adds that in her last job, "Several Millennials rejected promotions and said they 'saw what you go through and it's not worth it to me.'"

Millennials Want Opportunity

Across the board, every Millennial I talked with articulated a strong desire not to be stuck in a job with no future. The concept of "paying your dues" came up only three times in over one hundred interviews. Opportunity for growth and access was a constant theme for Millennials in and entering the workplace.

They want access to senior management. On a scale of one to ten (ten being high), access to senior management consistently scored nine or ten with every person age twenty-two to thirty-four I interviewed from across the country. Every single one.

This is a generation who has grown up one e-mail away from any CEO or political leader in the country or even the world. The notion that someone would be unavailable to them—or that it's okay for people in power to put a buffer between themselves and the people they lead—seems ridiculous.

Senior management are generally respected for their position, and their knowledge and experience is sought after. "I take things up the chain all the time," says Liz, if she can see how to get things done faster. She was quick to explain that she doesn't want to waste her time with middle managers who aren't accessible when she needs them to be or who "don't know how to help."

Most importantly, the power to advance or shortcut careers is clearly understood. "I have access to everyone, and I selectively go over people's heads because it gives me access to get knowledge, to networks, and to open doors," says Michael, twenty-seven, from New York City. "I used to take offense when people I manage went over my head, but I get it and know that it's not about me, it's about them" getting the access that will give them opportunity.

They want a strong mentor. Millennials understand the value of creating a network of experienced advisors who can help open doors, navigate a job search or situation in the work-place, and provide a helping hand during a career. While parents are the primary source of mentorship for Millennials, particularly recent college graduates, other experienced advisors willing to give some time to Millennials' worthy cause—themselves—are in high demand.

"We want to be mentored," says Caitlin, twenty-eight from Seattle. "Older workers have a lot of transferable knowledge and advice that will leave a big mark on the younger generation."

They want a career path. Following in Gen X's footsteps, Millennials don't see themselves as staying with one job or one company for their whole careers. They know that they need to take charge of their own careers, and they see a series of jobs as stepping-stones in the long yellow brick road of a career path. "They've always got their ears open to the next opportunity," says Leslie, the recruiter in San Francisco. To her it seems like everyone under thirty she has placed "is coming back around to (her) within nine to twelve months to find out if there's something better out there."

At the same time, the Millennials I talked with who were happy in their jobs talked expressively about how much potential they saw in their positions or their companies. "I feel there's a lot of room for growth at my company, and I'm really excited to see where it takes me," says Sally, summing up the sentiment.

Busting Millennial Myths

Taken together, how technology impacted how Millennials were raised, the input of their parents, and the mind-set that these phenomena yield paints a different picture from what has emerged in countless articles, books, conversations, forums, and blog comment sections. While it's easy to understand where the prevailing myths about Millennials and their work habits come from, we need to break down the myths

based on *their* upbringing, not ours, if we're going to successfully figure out how to productively collaborate and work with
them. Knowing what we know now, where does that leave us
with the prevailing myths?

Myth #1: Millennials are entitled. Busted: Millennials are
conditioned. They don't want anything we don't all desire!
They are us in younger bodies and with different parents. Millennials have been taught to expect certain conditions immediately that older workers had to wait for. To compound the
problem, their entry into the job market came at a terrible
time, economically.

**Myth #2: Millennials expect rewards and promotions for
showing up.** Plausible: They've gotten rewards for simple participation all along the way, so many don't know what mas-
tery looks like.

Myth #3: Millennials don't work hard. Busted: Millennials
work differently, and sometimes don't know what good work
is, which is not the same thing as "don't work hard."

Myth #4: Millennials can't get anything done. Busted: Millennials need context to get started and feedback to cross the
finish line, but their output can be phenomenal.

Myth #5: Millennials are casual and disrespectful. Half
busted/half plausible: As a culture, we are much less formal
in our dress than we were twenty, thirty, or forty years ago—
John F. Kennedy started the whole thing when he refused to
wear hats in 1960. Millennials have not been taught what
is appropriate in the workplace, and don't know how other,
older colleagues perceive them.

**Myth #6: Millennials want freedom, flexibility, and work–life
balance.** Split decision: Freedom? Some want the freedom to

be anywhere, while others value being in the office. Work–life balance? Confirmed: they have seen the compromised work–life mix that many Baby Boomers and Gen Xers have, and don't want it for themselves.

Now What?

So what's a tired forty-six-year-old who sees this and wants to call in sick tomorrow supposed to do? "Seriously, I worked this hard for this long, and this is what I have to deal with? I've earned the right to go into my office and shut the door," says Kate, forty-six, a general manager of a Boston-based marketing firm. The problem, according to Kate, is that it takes "a whole lot of energy to harness those demands in a constructive way. I've put my energy into getting here, and the game has changed. I'm all about servant leadership, but this is ridiculous. It never stops."

Here's the deal. We all need to do a few things to improve the workplace dynamic that seems to pit generation against generation. First: Boomers and Xers need to stop assuming every young person is the same. Millennials need to stop assuming everyone older than they are is out of touch and unproductive. Just as I don't want to be lumped in with the bad actors of my generation, Millennials don't want to be judged by a misunderstood perception about their generation.

Second: We need to get people over the first four years of their careers (whenever it really starts). The early twenties are a time of huge transformation, excitement, and uncertainty. It's always been hard to go from school, where the kid with straight As and the kid with the C average both advanced to the next grade despite their disparate achievements, to the workplace, where achievement rather than time is valued for advancement. This is not new. I am famous for saying in a 1991 interview with a potential employee, "I'm not going to be your *&^%ing babysitter." Yeah, I was a gem.

Third: Just because we didn't get what our younger

colleagues are asking for (okay, demanding) doesn't mean we shouldn't give it to them. Because we'll be giving it to ourselves too! Who doesn't want to understand how they fit into the bigger picture? Who doesn't want to be acknowledged for their contribution? Who doesn't want to matter? The challenge is not to stop these things from happening, the challenge is to move from assuming that everyone knows what to do to articulating expectations clearly and then maintaining them.

Fourth: Boomers and Xers can learn from younger colleagues. We Boomers and Xers need to meet our younger colleagues where they are and move them forward. At the same time, we all need to be open to learning from one another.

This doesn't mean that managers have to do all the work or not hold Millennials accountable. But managers do need to explain tasks and standards of work more concretely and consistently.

In the end, we will all be better off if we move some of our management styles around a bit and find ways of working together that benefit everyone.

PART 2

Making It Work at Work

4

Making Work Meaningful

"Just because" isn't going to work for me.
—Liz, age thirty

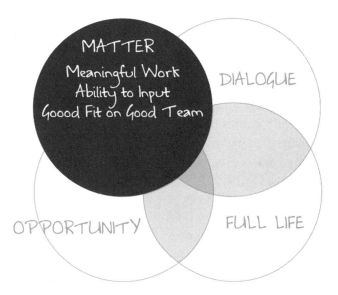

"Why can't they just do what I tell them to?"

Gone are the good old days, when "Because I told you to" was a useful or sustainable workplace tool. It might work once, but assume that icy stare or rolling of the eyes means that Joe is looking for a new job, and you'll soon be starting all over again training his replacement. And while it might seem better to replace the eye-roller, it's a costly slippery slope of extra time exiting one person and recruiting and onboarding a new one. And high turnover drives down productivity and morale.

The replacement cost is more than just the 16 to 20 percent of salary that is widely held as the estimated cost of turnover per person. Add your stress level and extra uncompensated hours to get the job done, and you can start to figure out the personal toll that replacing your team members before it is time takes on you.

Understanding the bigger picture is vital to getting started with a task, never mind doing the work well. Millennials have been conditioned to know that they can make a difference and that their presence is important. They want to understand how they make a difference in their work. And they want to be confident that what they do matters: that it matters to the team, to the company, to the bottom line, and to the vision. They want to understand how what seems mundane can possibly be important.

This, of course, flies in the face of what many older managers experienced as they moved up the ladder. "No one ever told me why I was doing the work—they just told me to do it, and I did," says Chris.

How dumb were we? Very.

I remember feeling bewildered about work tasks I didn't understand the relevance of, and when I figured it out—usually by myself—the lightbulb would go on and all of the sudden I'd be able to do things faster and better.

"My" Place Here

We all want to know how we fit into the big picture and what that big picture is. It's not enough to provide a clear vision for why our company exists, even though that is very hard to do well. Equally important is being able to describe what your team's role in that vision is, and how we each contribute to the team and therefore the vision. And you must reinforce this constantly.

Menial, entry-level work is the toughest to swallow for many recent college graduates. "It's a shock when they get a job and realize what entry-level really means," says Susan. "The attitude seems to be 'I don't want to do this' and 'I get it—and I want to do something important now.' And when reality hits them, they get bitter."

While earning your way up isn't dead, *not* understanding how and why bottom-level work fits into the bigger picture is a dead horse we can keep wasting our time beating, but it's not coming back to life. If you want a chance at keeping entry-level Millennials in the fold long enough for them to learn the ropes and become more productive and valuable to you, providing context for their jobs is critical, not optional.

What is this task for? Why does it matter? How does learning this task help with learning the next one? How is this not like calculus that you'll probably never use again? How does this stupid work fit into the more "important" work everyone else is doing? I'm going to say it now, and I'll say it again, you cannot overcommunicate this information for people from any generation, ever.

The Big Picture: Vision and Purpose

Unless you're on the founding team or are the CEO, you may not have had a role in creating the vision and mission for your company. But you should know it, breathe it, work it.

The business bookshelf is full of guides on creating a vision and mission that everyone can remember, embrace, and repeat. If you don't already have a clear mission in place, get one. Following are a few books that will help you articulate your business vision and mission:

- *The Story of Purpose* by Joey Reiman
- *It's Not What You Sell, It's What You Stand For* by Roy M. Spence Jr.
- *Start with Why* by Simon Sinek

My process is built on lots of years of helping companies articulate a compelling vision and mission that differentiates them from competitors in the category. And, because my brain is small, it's a pretty simple process that works for every kind of company, from retail operations to personal or corporate service firms, and from consumer packaged goods companies to religious institutions.

Answer these questions:

1. We work for: *interesting description of target market*
2. Who want/need to: *verb describing condition, desire, or need*
3. In a world that/where: *describe current condition you're solving for*

Example:

Acme Voice Talkers

We work for: *young boys struggling with severe speech disorders*
Who need to: *be able to communicate*
In a world where: *not being able to be understood significantly limits opportunity*

The Medium Picture: The Purpose of My Team

The big picture is not enough—teams need clarity on how their department or group fits into the big picture. And they need to know how their teams are a part of accomplishing the specific mission that's in front of them.

Answer these questions:

1. What does this department, group, or team do that is vital to the company?
2. If we weren't here what would happen?
3. If we weren't here what wouldn't happen?

My Picture: The Role of the Individual

Make sure your staff understands the value of their positions and how they fit into the larger whole. They should be able to answer these questions:

1. This job exists to:
2. *My* job is to make sure that:
3. If I wasn't here, this is what wouldn't happen:

This last step, the individual's immediate picture—why "I" make a difference—is critical. It may seem excessive, I know, but if people understand their purpose within the bigger vision, if they can tie their day-to-day work to making a difference, then work goes a bit smoother and more efficiently, with better output and good morale all the way around.

While we talk to outsiders and business partners about the company's big picture, we're better off talking to employees in terms of the pyramid's base being the person, not the company. It's true that we all ladder up to something bigger, but it's more effective to make the person the most "important" part of the pyramid when explaining how the work fits into the bigger purpose. This is true for Millennials as well as for those in your organization from other generations.

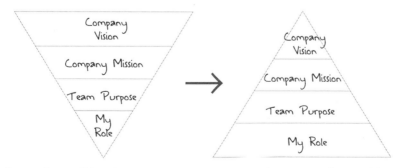

Invert the traditional pyramid for employees so they can understand how their work fits into the company's mission.

When managers talk with people individually, they should convey to each person how the different parts of his job ladder up to the company's reason for existing.

Sometimes people ask, "But Lee, doesn't this just feed into the problem?" No. This *cures* the problem. By creating a through line from individuals to the company vision and mission, you will give people a much clearer sense of why they, and by extension their work, matters.

Say it once, then say it again. Lather, rinse, and repeat. And repeat. And repeat.

How to Drive the Point Home

You may feel like a broken record (of course, some of your younger staff may not even know what that means) but you cannot overcommunicate what your company, your team, and each person is there to do, and what difference the person, the team, and the company will make in the world.

Use Onboarding to Introduce Purpose

Start at the beginning—day one, week one—with an onboarding process that includes an in-depth look at the company, the team, and the role. By the end of the first week, new employees should know more than where the water cooler is—they should be able to articulate how they fit into the team and how their work will advance the mission of the company.

Reset Teams with New People

When new people come onto your team, it's a good practice to reset the team so that everyone is clear on how the new person fits in. Take thirty minutes during a team meeting when you've added a new member to remind everyone about the vision and mission of the company, and how the team fits in. Show an organizational chart of how the team fits into the company or division. Detail the team's organizational chart so everyone has a clear view of how the new member adds to the strength of the team. Have each person articulate his role on the team so that the new person hears it—and so that team members reinforce what they know. Course correct if you need to, so no one leaves the meeting with a misconstrued idea of her own or someone else's role.

Expand Job Descriptions

Often, job descriptions focus exclusively on the job at hand and do not put the job in the context of the team. Expand your job descriptions so that each role is tied to a team's purpose and the company vision on paper. By including this context in the job description, you will make sure everyone understands how she fits in. (Don't forget to make sure that everyone has a copy of her job description.)

Provide Color and Context for Projects

"I never had to be told what was expected of me. Why don't they know, like we did?" asks Carol.

They don't. They just don't. Millennials have been overdirected since childhood, so many of them expect to be given guidelines; in the absence of those guardrails, they answer the question or complete the assignment in a shallow way that is often insufficient for the task at hand.

The primary source of dissonance in organizations is conflicting assumptions between and among teams and/or team members, regardless of age. How often do you hear comments like, "I didn't know that," "I thought I was supposed to..." or "Weren't you going to...?" Frustration is inevitable when we don't check assumptions and expectations and drive clarity into our language before the work starts. To be successful and efficient and to help make our teams successful and efficient, we need to meet them where they are, not do things that just continue to create disappointment and frustration.

While management consistently believes they have given clear, unambiguous direction, what many Millennials—and others on the team, for that matter—may hear are ambiguous, loose suggestions, creating recurring frustration for management.

I heard many versions of Andrew's complaint that if his manager had "only told me why the report mattered, and who it was going to, I would have done it differently." It shouldn't matter. But you can stop hitting your head against the wall and save yourself some time and a headache by just providing context every time you assign a project or task.

As you start new projects, do not assume that everyone understands the impetus for the project or his role in it. Take fifteen to twenty minutes at the beginning to talk through the full context and purpose of the project—discussing at the outset how each person will contribute and what the dependencies among people and tasks are saves a lot of time and questions later. E-mail this description to the whole team too, so if someone forgets you can refer her to the e-mail instead of stopping to explain again.

Boomer Advice: Mary, age fifty-four

"Now when I delegate, I take a much more collaborative approach. I take time to step back and explain the goals of the project, what I expect of each person, and how each assignment fits in with the others—more context and color is needed by this group before they get started."

Of course, you may get "I don't understand why it has to be done this way." Truthfully, I've learned that my people are finding better ways to do things all time. However, I ask them to do it my way once and *then* to suggest a different path to the same goal. This way, when they come back with new ideas I can talk with them about the specific steps and what they learned so I can be sure they understand the full context of the work at hand.

Once people of any generation understand how their work, however dull it may seem, matters to the team, they become more engaged, more active, and more thoughtful about it. Accountability increases when someone understands how his performance impacts the rest of the team's work and ultimately the office's or company's. Indeed, I've found that nothing conveys insufficient work more than the question "do you understand how you let the team down?"

All work matters, or you wouldn't need it to be done. Now it's just a question of making sure the people doing the work get it too.

Making a Difference Through Work Too

Beyond making a difference at work with meaningful work, Millennials want to make a difference through their work—in their communities and in the world at large—as well. Millennials want their companies to be active volunteers and contributors and to provide opportunities for them.

As reporter Laura Meckler articulated in *The Wall Street Journal*, Millennials "want to work for companies with public service missions. They want their employers to contribute to social and ethical causes." Meckler's bottom line, based in part on the work of Morley Winograd and Dr. Michael Hais who believe that Millennials are very likely to be steadfast in seeking to align their beliefs with their work, is exciting (for me) and cautionary for all of us: "[I]f the values of the Millennial generation hold up over time, corporate America may be in for a shock."And by corporate America, I think we mean *all* business: from the small business with fewer than ten employees, to the Fortune 100 with tens of thousands of people around the country. Companies that don't actively engage in their communities will be at a disadvantage in recruiting and retaining the strongest and broadest base of Millennials.

So there's no time like the present to jump in and articulate how your business will participate in the community: here's a few ways to jumpstart your thinking and doing:

1. Employee Match: Offer to match your employees' donations to non-profit organizations (by percentage of their total give or capped). You can decide to focus the company's giving in certain areas (sustainability, housing, food, etc. or leave it open).
2. Find one to three nonprofits that make the differences most aligned with your company mission and focus your company donations, time, and talent to advancing their causes.
3. Instead of gifts to your clients at the end of the year, donate to a nonprofit in their area in their names. At Double Forte, employees nominate different charities which we then vote on, and we donate the money we would have spent on client gifts to that winning organization in our clients' names.
4. Help your employees in their volunteer efforts. Many of your employees are active volunteers in a wide range of

worthy causes—there are lots of ways to help them help others. Offer up your office for committee meetings. Allow employees to e-mail the staff about volunteer opportunities with their charities (runs, clean up days, concerts etc.)

5. Focus team days on volunteer activities—use a service like VolunteerMatch to find great opportunities for your team to team-build while helping organizations in your community with team days that put your people to work where their ideas and elbow-grease are needed most.

Long-term you want a policy or framework and a budget (and you'll want to measure and report too!) but there's no time like the present to start making a bigger impact in your world now—and helping attract, retain, and excite your current and future employees.

Management Dos and Don'ts

- Do share your vision for your company, your team, and yourself—often. Explain how your company makes a positive difference.
- Do explain how everything you do is tied to the mission of the team and company. What may seem mundane is important—explain how and why.
- Do onboard new employees and new team members deliberately, taking the time to explain the vision and values of the company and how that new individual can make a difference.
- Do reset the team every time you add or lose a new person.
- Don't assume people understand how their role fits into the bigger picture.
- Don't assume that if you say it once it will sink in. You cannot—I repeat, you cannot—overcommunicate this stuff.
- Do save yourself a lot of time by taking the time at the beginning of any project to explain the purpose of the project and how each team member will contribute.

- Do actively engage in helping the community around you: find ways to help your employees regularly help worthy organizations.

Millennial Dos and Don'ts

- Do know that no one is going to employ you for work that doesn't matter.
- Do ask how you fit in, if you don't know.
- Do perform tasks your supervisor's way at least once before you suggest a new way.
- Don't assume leadership knows all the technical shortcuts you do; be prepared to show others when you describe new ways of doing things so they can understand that you're not cutting corners.
- Do come ready for your first week with the questions you need to understand the role you've just accepted.
- Do participate in your company's volunteer activities. If your company does not have volunteer activities, find your own and seek ways to engage your team.

5

Soliciting Input

Anyone who has an idea is heard...I finally found the right job.

—Liz, age thirty

Hand in hand with wanting work that matters is a consistent desire among Millennials to be able to contribute right now to the shape of the business. And they also want to contribute any ideas they have—which, I promise you, is a good thing. We want engaged employees; when people find their ideas are used, they become more engaged; when managers see more engaged employees, they are more likely to give those employees more authority and responsibility. It's a positive circle of energy that builds goodwill, productivity, and morale.

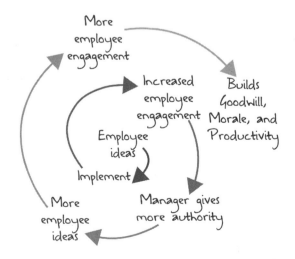

Millennial Insight: Anonymous, age twenty-nine

"I wish management would stop using age in place of experience and different points of view that we [Millennials] have. In today's tech/social world Millennials have the experience of living the demographic and the user. While the Gen Xers and Baby Boomers are older, they don't often ask Millennials for input on something. Millennials want to feel invested in a project's success, so asking them to be part of the process, and for their points of view and suggestions, will instill in them a sense of ownership."

Asking for input is easy to do, yet it is hard to do well.

The most important thing about soliciting ideas is making sure you loop back and tell people what you did with their thoughts. Nothing squelches enthusiasm more than letting that enthusiasm disappear into a big black hole of unresponsiveness. If you are not willing to explain what you are (or are not) doing with people's suggestions, then it'd be better if you didn't ask for input. Of course, don't expect young people to stick around. In fact, don't expect anyone really good to stick around.

"Every time I suggested a change in the work flow, I was told that I wasn't allowed to give input on how to do my job or how the work would be divided in the team," says Madison. "I had to get out of there."

Mary describes how her last company couldn't keep any of the "really talented" Millennials they had hired over a three-year period, because these young employees were not listened to: "Once they realized they weren't able to give ideas that would actually be used, they'd leave." According to Mary, the company had a revolving door of great young people who consistently, six to nine months after they were brought in, would "flame out" because the company couldn't figure out what to do with them or their ideas.

In her new position, Mary has built in time so her younger staff members can have a bigger voice in the process: "It takes longer up front, but we get lots of good ideas and everyone is happier when they start the projects, even if we can't use all of the ideas that people suggest. It's made a huge difference in morale and productivity compared to my last job."

Get Feedback Day to Day

While soliciting input may seem like an invitation to disaster if you're not accustomed to it, the positive energy you will create by doing so is priceless. And input need not be chaotic: a little structure goes a long way to productively engaging your team in the what and how you do things.

Be Open to New Ideas

"How can we do this better?" should not just be on the tip of every manager's tongue, it should be hanging in the air after it's been spoken.

We can't assume that a process we learned five, never mind fifteen, years ago hasn't been improved! It's probably been improved four or five times by now. The people closest to the work and newest to the organization may look at our processes with the incredulity of savvy wielders of technology, social tools, and services. Of course, they don't have the benefit of institutional history. So how do we meld the two?

I ask that every new person learn the way we're doing something so he can see the steps we take to reach certain milestones or granularity. After the new team member has done something once, it's okay to propose ways of streamlining the process or improving the outcome.

The beginning of projects is a perfect time to solicit ideas on the desired outcome, process, or methods. Here you can learn a lot about how well your team is prepared for the task at hand. Sit on your hands if you have to, so that you don't tell people what to do! After you've laid out the goals of a program, set a time a couple of days later for people to come together again to share their ideas about how to proceed.

Workshop the program instead of dictating it. Using a coaching leadership style at the front end of a project offers the perfect opportunity for the team to provide input and for you to hear new ideas and help instead of dictate. Following are questions you can ask to get the group moving in the right direction:

- How would you approach this?
- What timeline do you think will help meet the deadline without having to rush at the end?
- What else do we need to know?
- What can we get started on now?
- How do you see the team conquering and dividing?
- What kind of elements do you think we should include in this project? How do they build on each other?

Listen to it all. Let people surprise you.

Think about this process as providing care on the front end instead of triage on the back end. You may have to redirect people. However, with this approach you will most likely have engaged teammates who are more invested in the outcome and the process than they would be if you simply dictated the steps, elements, and timeline. And if some people don't engage and then complain later, you have a perfect stage for resetting their expectations on how to participate.

At the end of projects, get input from the team on what they learned that they could apply the next time to make the process easier, better, or more efficient. When ideas come up, put a plan in place to put them into action. As you go through the "new" way, assess how it's working: Did the team get what it wanted? Is the person or people who came up with the new process happy with the result? How can we further tweak it to improve? Often we move so quickly from project to project that we fail to take a moment and think about what could have gone better or what we could have done differently. (More on double-loop and single-loop learning in chapter 9.)

Be Available

Encourage people to bring their ideas forward. Offer office hours or open invitations for those who are in open-plan offices so that it's easy for people to bring ideas to you. If someone comes forward: listen, triage, and follow up.

Unless it's an urgent issue, don't feel like you need to instantly act on an idea. Articulate a way forward so that the person knows you're taking the idea seriously. If you know you can't act on it in the next three months, say so. Tell the person to loop back with you in a defined time frame to revisit the idea. After the meeting, e-mail that person and thank him for bringing the idea forward—if you're not that person's manager, loop the manager in so she knows what's come up and can help either move the idea forward or manage expectations with her employee.

Some ideas are easy! I overheard someone in the kitchen say how much her team likes iced tea, and voilà, we had an iced tea maker the next day: it's a $40 investment that we use every day. Our office manager noticed that many people were mixing protein shakes in the morning, but couldn't get them as smooth as they wanted. One Silver Bullet blender later, and everyone has a smooth shake. That was a pretty inexpensive and easy way to make the kitchen a bit better.

Other ideas are harder to implement but pay off in spades. One Double Forte employee came forward with an idea that would allow everyone on the staff to get more opportunities to practice presenting in front of a large group. Now we reserve five to ten minutes of each weekly staff meeting for a short presentation by a staff member. Everyone takes a turn and puts together a presentation that he creates, practices, and presents. To help people get more comfortable giving and receiving feedback, two other staff members give positive reinforcement and constructive suggestions for improvement to the presenter after each staff meeting. One idea, two birds killed: improved performance.

Get People to Participate

Our office is in a hermetically sealed office building with acoustic tiles and triple-pane windows. When no one's talking, it is like being in a Kleenex box, and all you can hear is typing. To put some energy into the air, we installed an audio system and have a low volume of music playing all day long in the background.

Every week we randomly select five people who choose a Pandora or Spotify music station or provide their playlists from their phones or iPods for the office background music. They can choose whatever they like, within reason, which leaves 99 percent of all options open to people: no NSFW soundtracks, no lullabies, no explicit-warning songs. Everyone gets a turn.

Happy Hour is Friday, around 3:30 p.m. Each week a different person chooses a beverage (alcohol-based and its nonalcoholic companion) for everyone to enjoy.

Every workplace has events or traditions that everyone can participate in or take turns leading. Find yours and get everyone involved.

Get Feedback Annually

Do you really know what your employees think? Do you know how happy or engaged they are with their jobs and the company? Do they like the culture? Would they like to introduce something new into the office? Are they proud to work there?[1] I'm going to say no, you don't know.

Plan to solicit real input from everyone in the company once a year. Use online survey tools such as SurveyMonkey.com or KwikSurveys.com so that gathering feedback and tabulating answers is simple for the employees and for you.

Survey Steps

1. Plan a survey of thirty-five to forty questions that takes no more than thirty minutes to answer (unless someone has a lot to say), and use a mix of qualitative, open-ended questions and quantitative questions that ask people to rate their opinions on a five-point scale. (Sample questionnaires available at leecaraher.com.)

2. Make sure you ask demographic questions such as age range, gender, location, and job status (e.g., full-time, part-time, contractor, seasonal, etc.) so you can group the answers and find trends among different groups. As Tim Donnelly, freelance writer for *Inc. Magazine*[2] says, "Most surveys will inquire as to whether the employee has a good work–life balance, whether they are proud to work for the organization, and how much effort they put into their work."

3. Make your survey anonymous with the option of providing a name—this helps ensure the most candid feedback possible.

4. Give your team two weeks do the survey, and choose a time outside your busiest months. During the two weeks, keep people updated on survey tracking numbers, encouraging people to fill it out.

5. Within two to three weeks after the survey closes, bring the broad learnings and trends forward. Identify any immediate action plans or long-term projects you are considering, so that people know you're taking the input seriously. It would be

too bad to get great ideas, implement them, and not let anyone know the impact they've had.

Brainstorms

Brainstorming is a great way to kill one, two, or more good ideas, and demotivate your team. Truly.

In our rush to get the answers we need to get the job done, we sometimes unintentionally squash good ideas—and the environment that encourages them—as soon as they start. "I stopped participating in brainstorms. Our manager doesn't want to hear my ideas—he just wants to have gone through the process so he can say he did," says Mariah, twenty-six.

Stop trying to problem solve in a brainstorming session. The point is to get as many ideas as possible on the board—think forty to sixty ideas—so that you can workshop them in a smaller group and whittle them down to the one or two ideas that your team will take forward.

Next time you plan a brainstorm, choose someone on your team to lead a small-group idea session. Coach the person beforehand on what you want to get out of the session and what information people will need in order to generate relevant ideas. Have the leader plan a five-minute icebreaker at the beginning of the session, to provide a break from whatever people have been working on and get them into a mode of creative thinking and idea generation.

Other resources to help you generate great ideas from people in the office include:

- *Creative Confidence: Unleashing the Creative Potential Within Us All* by Tom Kelley and David Kelley
- *Visual Meetings: How Graphics, Sticky Notes & Idea Mapping Can Transform Group Productivity* by David Sibbet

Ask for Fully Formed Ideas

Ideas—shared and not shared—about how to improve the work environment, a process, or an outcome are everywhere, floating around in thought bubbles over people's heads as they go through the day. One way to encourage responsible "complaining" is to require that ideas be accompanied by a project plan.[3]

"Ideas are fine," says Brian Klapper, president and founder of the Klapper Institute, "but you want submitters to go further, presenting a simplified project plan. That forces them to strengthen weaker ideas by dealing with the practical aspects of implementation. You're not after a fancy, multipage business plan, but a clear indication of objectives, competitive advantages offered, degrees of difficulty to implement, estimated timelines, costs, and revenues, size of the team needed to implement, and a risk assessment."

Soliciting input from colleagues, putting good ideas into play, and tweaking to improve them will not only improve your work but also the morale of the group.

Management Dos and Don'ts

- Do keep an open mind to ideas no matter where they come from. Just because Millennials don't have a lot of experience doesn't mean they don't have good ideas.
- Do loop back with individuals and groups to let them know where their idea stands. If the idea can't be implemented now, say so, and encourage them to keep the ideas coming.
- Don't ever say, "You're too young to know…" unless you want people beating a path to the exit door.
- Do encourage people to think through their ideas before they present them.
- Do conduct an audit or survey of your team or company once a year to get a good look at what's going on.

- Do show people how to do things, and then be ready to get their input on how to make things better.
- Do let other people lead brainstorms.

Millennial Dos and Don'ts

- Do give your ideas in a constructive way—put together a detailed project plan for your idea before you take it to the boss.
- Do tasks their way the first time, and *then* suggest changes—sometimes things are done in a particular way for reasons you may not be able to see until you do them.
- Do know that not everything can be implemented right away.
- Do fill out surveys honestly and thoughtfully.

6

A Good Fit on a Good Team

Fit matters.

—*Lee Caraher*

"Fit," that amorphous notion describing how well we meld with a team or company's culture, is consistently listed as an important element by Millennials when discussing why a position is a good one or not. While I understand that chemistry in the laboratory is an exact science, it's more an art form in the workplace.

I learned this the hard way. When I was in my thirties, I figured out that bad fit was affecting my outlook and my happiness and, most importantly, my bottom line. Fit is now an important business filter through which we view all potential employees and potential clients. After "only take a client if someone other than Lee is interested in the work," rule number two in client vetting: Don't take the client unless the fit is good—there should be a chemistry match, a culture match, and a values match.

Millennials have watched their parents negotiate their own work lives, and they know already that they don't want to work with people they don't respect or want to spend time with. What took me more than fifteen years to implement Millennials now want at the beginning of their careers. "The team around me matters a lot," says Jennifer, age twenty-nine. "People want to work around people they like, that make them better, who work well together. We want to have good relationships with all of the people we work with."

One recruiter describes a call she got from a person she had placed in a job. On the new employee's first day at the company, the recruiter says, "She called me in the early afternoon and said, 'These people are not a good fit for me, how could you place me here? Don't you know who I am?' This was after four separate day-long interviews at the company and a long screening test."

Sorting out fit starts with knowing what your company's values are and what your culture really is. It's also important to show people how they can fit in now and in the future.

What are your company's or your team's values? Do you know? Does your team know? Would everyone give the same answer, if asked?

Values need to be declared, socialized, and reinforced. And they need to be explained: How would someone work within the values of your office regarding the way they collaborate with colleagues, hold a standard of work, communicate with customers, and service clients? If your team doesn't have clear values, this is the time to cocreate them, so that you can improve the way people work together and better determine who fits into your company as you grow and change.

Define Company Values

There are as many ways to go about defining and declaring values as there are leaders. The most important piece of declaring company values, however, is including everyone in the process. Cocreating company values with your teams ensures that people really understand what those values mean and how team members bring them to life and are invested in them (or not).

Besides cocreation, common tenets in the methods I have used—both in my own company and in helping clients do this important work—are:

1. Include everyone in the discovery process.
2. Identify and synthesize four to six commonly held beliefs.

3. Use memorable phrases to describe your values. "Excellence" is trite if you can't describe what it means specifically to your organization.
4. Define how you will know if the company and the people are living and working within the values.
5. Define how you will socialize and reinforce the values so they are constantly communicated and part of the social fabric of the team.

When you are recruiting, try to sort out fit before someone (young or more mature) starts his first day on the job. Be prepared to help the people who are a poor fit *not* apply and to help the people who will be attracted to the position apply and rise to the top of the stack. Start by putting your company's or team's values into all of your job descriptions. Do everything you can to convey in the job description the culture, what matters in the office, and the way people work together.

Zappos Leading the Way

"Hire slow, fire fast" sounds good but is challenging to put into action. Zappos.com, the online shoe and apparel store now owned by Amazon, regards fit as so important that it pays people $3,000[1] to leave after four weeks if the new employees don't think they're a good fit—no harm, no foul. This practice weeds out the people who are driven by values different than Zappos' and the people who have bought into Zappos' culture are left behind to contribute to the team. It's probably the boldest HR recruiting and onboarding policy to support a culture and productivity in the history of business.

Zappos values:

1. Deliver Wow Through Service
2. Embrace and Drive Change

3. Create Fun and a Little Weirdness
4. Be Adventurous, Creative, and Open-Minded
5. Pursue Growth and Learning
6. Build Open and Honest Relationships with Communication
7. Build a Positive Team and Family Spirit
8. Do More with Less
9. Be Passionate and Determined
10. Be Humble

Personality Matters

Remember that one person's star is another's misfit. For example, someone who likes to work alone and then report in won't fit well in a team that works collaboratively in person and crowdsources its ideas and decisions from the group.

Think about who is on your team and who else you might need to round it out. Everyone has strengths and weaknesses, abilities and opportunities, and natural tendencies. Understanding the different personalities or profiles on the team not only helps people work together better, it also helps determine strengths the team lacks. Filling these gaps on the team when you make new hires improves efficiency and productivity.

Consider adopting a personality indicator system that helps everyone understand themselves and one another better. Once understood, these can help you make adjustments to maximize everyone's contributions.

A couple of years ago, everyone at my company completed the Myers-Briggs Type Indicator[2] (MBTI) and the Strength Finders[3] assessment, and assembled and shared our team profiles based on the results of these tests. It was enlightening in so many ways.

Most startling, we discovered that fully half of the staff are introverts, people who work better by absorbing information, mulling it over, and then responding. This is in stark contrast to extroverts, who often work well in the moment.

It's unusual in a public relations and marketing firm to have more than 20 or 30 percent of the company test as introverts, and we have fully 50 percent of the people testing not just as introverts, but as strong introverts. And 12 percent of our people throughout the organization are INFJs, which make up only 1 to 3 percent of the general population.

With this information in hand, we looked at some of our processes and figured out quickly that some of the things we were doing, including the way we were approaching brainstorming, were best suited for extroverts. Wake-up call! I set up the company to work for me, a strong E[xtrovert] NFP—no wonder some people felt like they weren't contributing as much as they could.

We also have several ESTJs, strong personalities that can be perceived as insensitive unless they are understood on teams with their opposite types, INFPs and ISFPs. While everyone liked and respected one another, the two groups were having a hard time understanding why the other couldn't see their point of view. With the MBTI types and Strength Finders results in hand, we were able to bridge the divide between the types and to more readily tap into different people's innate strengths as well as minimize areas in which they are less strong.

Today, we tackle projects at the outset to suit different types so everyone is better set up for success. One thing we do differently now is prepare for brainstorm sessions earlier so that the introverts in the group can think about the topic ahead of time and then contribute more fully during the session. Adding one to two days of preparation and thinking time has dramatically improved our sessions.

Other companies use the DISC personality assessment based on the work of William Marston, Walter Clarke, and John Geier. The DISC model measures personality based on four categories—D: Dominance, I: Influence, S: Steadiness, and C: Compliance.[4] A considerable amount of work has been done on the best type of DISC profile to fill different roles and jobs in companies. For instance, for salespeople, choose people with high D (driver) and high I (influence); for accountants, choose people with high C (compliance) and S (security).

Whichever way you decide to assess people's personalities and work styles, pursue a model and implement it. It will help you and your team work better together and recruit people who fit your team well.

Recruiting the Next Team Member

Sort out as many cultural misfits as you can on the phone, before they get into the office for an interview. Unless you value having your own Island of Misfit Toys, doing this ahead of the interview phase saves both you and them a great deal of time and effort.

In our company the set of criteria is pretty straightforward. At Double Forte, we are looking for:

- Initiative takers
- Those who are demonstrably curious
- Team players
- People who can write two lucid, compelling paragraphs together
- Those with a sense of humor (if you don't like to laugh along, you definitely won't be happy at Double Forte)

In the prescreen, focus a chunk of time on questions that elicit responses about how your candidates work and what they value. Include questions such as:

1. What type of work environment are you are most comfortable in?
2. What makes you happy about your work?

3. What are the characteristics of the best boss you've had, or the one you wish you'd had?
4. What are your expectations about the team you'll be working with?
5. Where do you see yourself in two years?

Of course, if you're interviewing Millennials just entering the workforce without any previous work experience, then you'll need to focus on character questions that get to work style.

Once you've got a young candidate in for an interview, be prepared to answer questions like, "Why would I want to work here?" "What are the teams like?" and "What's the mentorship program?"

While we might find these off-putting and presumptuous, try not to let them get in the way. These inexperienced, young adults have probably been steered this way by their parents or their uninformed friends. If they make it past the interview with you, give them pointers for their interview with the team.

Leigh, an in-house recruiter at a large entertainment company, says, "Once my candidates get past the first screen, I really put them through the paces about how to get through the in-person interviews. What to wear. What to ask. How to answer questions so they don't sound entitled. Some great candidates take hours of work to get them prepared for a successful interview. And if we're successful, they end up having a much better entry than the candidates that don't reframe their expectations."

Let the team interview the prospective employee—perhaps by going to lunch or having coffee together. As much as the candidate wants to know whom she might work with, the team should have the opportunity to understand who's in the mix for open positions. Ultimately, making the team dynamic positive matters more to the existing employees more than it does to the prospective ones.

Make sure your team is well versed in how to conduct themselves in interviews (for example, don't ask questions about race, age, family, and so on). Team members should offer feedback in as uniform and constructive a way as possible. As much as you can, discourage people from talking together in public about any candidate.

Consider a simple form that ranks a candidate on five factors:

Cultural Fit #1 (Choose one factor to asses, for example, attitude, work style, team player)	1 2 3 4 5	Comments:
Cultural Fit #2 (Choose a second factor to assess)	1 2 3 4 5	Comments:
Experience (Is the candidate's experience right for the open position)	1 2 3 4 5	Comments:
Specific Job Requirement #1 (Choose one requirement to assess here)	1 2 3 4 5	Comments:
Specific Job Requirement #2 (Choose another to assess)	1 2 3 4 5	Comments:

This way all of your team members can weigh in on the candidate in a constructive way.

Advice for Candidates of All Ages

Interviewing for a new job with people you don't know is daunting; you are up against an unknown number of other people. While an interview is as much for you as it is for the potential employer, take these steps to make sure you use the time to showcase your talent and solicit information about the position without hurting your chances.

- Please, don't ask questions like, "Why should I work here?" or "What do you have to offer me?" I know that's what you're thinking, but don't do it—you will be black-balling yourself before you've had a chance.
- Don't just talk about how great you are. Be ready with intelligent questions about the company, the team, and the position. Read the company website before you go in. Do a news search on the company and its key players before the interview. Know what job you're applying for.
- Do match the dress code "plus one" for interviews. If this is a casual office and everyone's in T-shirts and flip flops, wear a cool button-down shirt and clean casual shoes. If it's a professional casual office, wear a suit, no tie. Ladies, opt for closed-toe shoes until you know the policy. You get the idea.
- If you are left in a conference room or office to wait for your interviewer, don't forget to stand up to shake your interviewer's hand when she comes in. Take your sunglasses off your head as soon as you walk in the building. Drop the coffee cup and/or spit out the gum before you go into the building.
- Your interview starts as soon as you go through the door: be courteous to the receptionist and assistant—their reactions may be the deciding factor for you getting to the next level.
- Send a written thank-you note to everyone you met with, articulating why you'd like to be on the team and conveying your appreciation for their time.
- Parents: stay home. Do not call. Do not negotiate for your children. You are hurting your child's chances, even at parent-friendly offices.
- Turn off your phone before the interview. If you forget to turn it off and it rings, silence it immediately and apologize.

Xer Battle Scar: Kris, forty-five

"I will never forget a twenty-one-year-old young (emphasis on young) woman I was interviewing for a marketing coordinator position. She was a University of California, Berkeley graduate and had an impressive internship on her résumé. That is where my admiration ended. Coffee in hand, she waltzed into my office, dropped her bag on the floor, and perched her sunglasses atop her head before collapsing into a chair. At one point she did put her coffee down, on my desk, in order to wave her arms around as a visual aid in her explanation of how impressive she was. Needless to say, I didn't hire her."

Protect Your Culture

Once new people roll onto your team, pay close attention to the team's dynamics. Are people getting along? Are they working well together? Is the work product what you expected?

Use a thirty-, sixty-, and ninety-day check-in schedule to get a good handle on how your new team member is doing and what the team dynamics are like after the honeymoon is over and people aren't as conscious about being on their best behavior.

Are there team communication conventions that the new person hasn't gotten the hang of yet? Does the new person seem clear about his direction? Is he meeting deadlines? Is he on track with the work you expected? Show people exactly what you expect, so that the team keeps moving forward.

As Eion, a thirty-four-year-old CEO of a multinational service software company says, "Protect your culture at all costs. Everyone wants to be part of a great team, but not everyone is a good team match for our culture. If someone doesn't fit, they need to go."

Management Dos and Don'ts

- Do define and socialize your company values so everyone can live them.
- Do understand the team you have. Use Myers-Briggs, Strength Finders DISC, or another assessment tool so everyone can understand themselves and each other better and adjust accordingly.
- Do identify key cultural attributes for new team members and hire with them in mind.
- Do involve multiple people in the interview process; solicit constructive input of the candidates from everyone.
- Do protect your culture.

Millennial Dos and Don'ts

- Do put your best foot forward in interviews by being prepared.
- Do be able to articulate your values about work.
- Do not lead with work–life balance in any question about your work aspirations.
- Do remember it's NOT about you – it's about how you fit in with whoever is already there.

7

Meaningful Acknowledgment and Appreciation

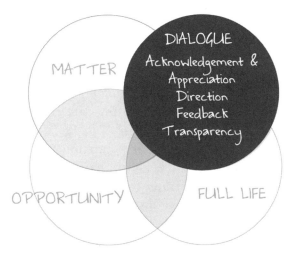

Teams who feel appreciated outperform those who don't.
—*Lori Ogden Moore, executive coach*

My elder son's room used to be full of medals, trophies, certificates, gold stars, and other evidence that he partici-pated in soccer, choir, school, camp, and more. Most of them were for simply showing up, framed and mounted (by me) as a continually growing shrine to his worth. When he decided to focus on music, all evidence of participation in other activi-ties was either thrown away by him (or rescued by me). What remains today are a few mementos that matter to him as evidence of his musical journey. My teenage son is focused that way. (I still have buckets of the other stuff that I will one day sort through when I have time—my guess is that 90 percent of it will end up in the dumpster.)

Every parent I talked with about this trophy phenomenon laughed out loud when I asked about their trophy "walls"—which ranged from refrigerators, actual walls, and special cases to scrapbooks and digitally produced memory books full of photos of the exact moments the honors were bestowed. Parents who have yet to touch their out-of-the-house grown children's rooms talked either from a point of pride in the accomplished children they raised or with a bit of embarrassment that they hadn't cleaned those rooms out yet. One parent of a twenty-five-year-old said, "I still have the 'My Child is an Honor Student' bumper sticker on my car, and my daughter graduated from college two years ago."

One generalization that gets lots of airtime in the media, on blogs, and in the comment fields of articles posted online is that Millennials have grown up with medals, trophies, certificates, and gold stars given for just showing up, and are used to the continual praise and reinforcement heretofore reserved for actual achievement. Everyone-wins soccer games. Trophies of all sizes for participation regardless of win-loss ratio. Inflated grades that neither give a true measure of comprehension nor a reason to get discouraged. All of these are common phenomena that set parents' heads nodding and managers' teeth grinding.

In contrast, my father, now seventy-five, often says, "Please and thank you are implied," to which my now-deceased mother would take varying degrees of umbrage, depending on how many implications had already been made that day.

Millennials have been conditioned to expect acknowledgment and appreciation all the time, and it can be exhausting trying to keep up with that expectation if you don't already have an authentic appreciation culture that reinforces good team collaboration and acknowledges valuable achievement.

"We find that many Millennials are somewhat needy in terms of wanting constant recognition for what senior management thinks of as 'regular work,'" says Mark, fifty-four and a senior vice president in a large consumer products company. "It's a very different expectation of recognition than we had at that early stage of our careers."

Gratuitous appreciation has no place in the workplace. Authentic appreciation is the only valuable appreciation; it's the only beneficial reinforcement that Millennials, and the rest of us, can learn from.

Millennial Insight: Carl, age twenty-six

"As a Millennial, the most important aspect to me is employee treatment and appreciation. This can be seen in many forms; however, I see it in compensation and work–life balance. In a society where the expectation is working fifty hours for a forty-hour paycheck, this 'should' be the most important to a Millennial. I don't want to receive e-mail on my personal phone, provide my phone number to my employer, or be 'pressured' into taking a wellness class for $60 a week extra. I want to have the option to 'unplug' for the day, not be bothered during my personal time, and not be penalized on an annual review because I don't lead any organizations. I want to put in 100 percent while working, go home and have a drink with my significant other. That is what is most important to me."

Appreciation Isn't Just for Millennials

Establishing a culture of true appreciation and acknowledgement that reinforces contribution rather than simple presence is the key to shifting expectations away from appreciation for everyday tasks and behavior. Instead, teach people to feel, and know, that they and their work are truly valued in the organization.

It may seem frivolous and enabling at the outset, however building an appreciative culture has been shown to improve performance empirically for the entire team. Organizations built on a culture of recognition have "14 percent better employee engagement, productivity, and customer service"[1] than those teams where regular recognition is rare. And when measuring customer satisfaction, profitability, and internal efficiencies and workflows, the most effective teams are the ones that have more positive interactions: three positive comments to one negative comment are necessary to encourage the most successful functioning.[2]

An appreciative culture starts at the top and gets reinforced by peer-to-peer acknowledgement. "If you're in a leadership position, you set the tone for those around you," says Paul, fifty-five, partner of a midsized law firm. "Not only does the person in charge need to be appreciative, he or she needs to set the expectation that everyone will be appreciative to each other, and show them how it's done."

The Power of Please and Thank You

Thank you. These two small words, when spoken (or typed or written), make a *big* difference in your day—whether you are saying or hearing them.

At work, do we have to say "Thank you?" I guess, technically, no—it's work, it's supposed to be done. We're supposed to collaborate, we're supposed to get work done, and we're supposed to do it well. Many of the older set in the office may echo the sentiment Terry expressed, "When I was their age, I knew that my paycheck was my thank you."

Or they think like *Mad Men*'s Don Draper:

Don: That's how this works. I pay you for ideas.
Peggy: You never say "Thank you."
Don: That's what the money is for![3]

I'm here to tell you that the more we say "please" and "thank you," the better people feel about their contributions, which improves morale, which contributes to a positive work environment, which, in turn, improves performance and increases talent longevity. "Thank you" goes a long way.

Francesca Gino of Harvard University and Adam Grant of the Wharton School researched the topic, and it turns out that most of us "don't realize how powerful it is to say thank you...and the effects are large. And they're important."

Maybe people don't say thank you in the workplace because, as Martin Kilduff of University College London suggests, leaders and managers are supposed to help other people achieve. But if we just get over that and acknowledge the help with a thank you, the bestower of thanks also gets a big benefit to himself. Gino explains the results of many studies that show that the bestowers of thanks "experience all sorts of positive emotions. They're more attentive, alert, energetic, and happy about life in general."

Thank people for what they're doing. Ask them with a "please" somewhere in the sentence when you want or need them to do something. You'll be spreading good feelings for the team and for yourself.

I can hear the collective sigh now. "But, Lee, 'thank you' gets misconstrued, and if I say thank you they will expect a raise or a promotion."

You might fear that, or you might have been told that, but it's not a realistic workplace expectation and you need to explain that to people of any age who don't get it.

Here's the deal. We need to lay out our expectations for our workplace and company culture. We need to explain that "thank you" and "please" are courteous and expected but do not indicate that a raise or a promotion are in order. (In contrast, *not* using "please" and "thank you" should prevent a raise or a promotion.) We need to make sure we don't avoid hard conversations about expectations and reality, so that "thank you" and "please" don't show up in a vacuum of positive-only feedback that gives people a lopsided under-standing of their own performance. (Feedback is covered in the next chapter, so hang on for that.)

Some managers complain that no one ever says "thank you" or "please" to them: "I give and I give and I give, and I get nothing back," says Brian, forty-seven, of his twenty-plus-person team, most of whom are under age thirty.

If you've laid out your expectations of an appreciative culture, you consistently reinforce it in your own workday, and you're not getting something back from certain people on your team, then it may be time for the non-reciprocators to go.

Before you show them to the door, I encourage you to have the hard one-on-one conversation to:

- Discuss what's expected
- Listen to the feedback the person may have for you
- Articulate exactly how you'd like the employee to show up, and
- Come up with mutual agreements about a way forward

It takes practice and it takes persistence, but in the end it's worth it—you either get an improved situation or you get rid of someone who's not going to fit your culture.

What does "thank you" look like? Of course, it's not useful if "thank you" becomes simply a game, like watching Peyton Manning play football and taking a swig every time he says "Omaha." However, if you imagine speech "bubbles" over your team, it would be wonderful to see many of them filled with some form of the word.

The Expression

What are some of the words and phrases your team should be using to convey their appreciation for one another?

- Thank you
- Thanks
- Merci
- I appreciate it
- I'm grateful

Mean it. Look the person in the eye.

When should you use one of these expressions of gratitude? Any time someone brings you something, agrees to something, gives you something, helps you, or delivers her assignment early or on time. When someone brings you a coffee, a printout from the printer, your lunch, their report, and after a meeting, make sure to thank him.

"You're welcome" is the appropriate response to "thank you" *every time,* to acknowledge that you've been thanked.

The E-Mail Thank-You

Use some form of "please" somewhere in the sentence when giving direction or making a request. Likewise, use some form of "thank you" as the sign-off when sending a request or direction.

Thanks in e-mail—here's what it looks like:

- Thanks
- Thanks so much
- Thank you
- I appreciate your help

Resist the urge to shortcut this by putting it into your e-mail signature. Type out the eight letters and a space—the effort will be appreciated, or at least you won't be derided for a lame automatic reply.

Example:

Hi Adam,

Can you please (or "I'd appreciate it if you could" or "I need you to please") move up the sales report to deliver to Joe by Tuesday at 10, instead of Wednesday, as originally planned? Meetings have moved and we want to have enough time to get feedback so we're all on the same page before the board meeting. Let me know if I can help you or if you need to move something else off your plate to accommodate this.

Thanks,

John

When applicable, start e-mails off on a positive note by thanking the recipient for what he's already done.

Example:

- Thank you for your prompt reply
- Thanks for bringing this to my attention
- Thank you for the information
- Thanks for taking the time

Thanks in Company Instant Messaging Platform

The beauty of instant messaging (IM) is that we can have less formal, quick back-and-forth conversations with people spread out geographically (or way across the room—but please don't IM the person sitting next to you to ask her something!).

The challenge with IM is that we can go back and forth with such speed and shorthand that the "please" and "thank you" get lost. First, if you're going back and forth more than four or five times, stop typing and pick up the phone. Second, use thank you at the end of the interaction—just do it. Don't leave the other person hanging, wondering if you're finished or not.

If you work in an emoticon-friendly culture, use the smiley face or some other appropriate symbol to convey your thanks. Personally, I love emoticons, but have been known to overdo it with people who aren't as enamored as I am. If you do use emoticons, refrain from using them with people outside your organization.

Thanks in Text Messages

Millennials aren't the only ones texting their way through the day. A lot of work dialogue is happening between phones. Because texting is shorthand and can be easily misinterpreted, texting "thank you" is even more important. When texting, end every exchange with "Thanks." Speed things up by creating a "shortcut tx" that generates "Thanks" in the text box if you want to save keystrokes. Or use an emoticon to say thanks, so that the person you're texting knows that you got her agreement or information.

"Are you kidding me?" you're thinking. "Did you just dedicate three pages to showing people how to say and write please and thank you?" Yes, yes, I did. How do I know this is necessary? It's the first thing we need to teach interns or entry-level people to do. When I've blogged on the topic I get endless comments. My clients and colleagues in my peer network tell me again and again that they have the same issue.

Many Millennials have grown up with digital communication norms that have eliminated please and thank you from the dialogue. E-mail, texts, and instant messages are by their nature informal—and everyone of every age can be accused of getting sloppy and being misinterpreted, causing communication missteps easily avoided by remembering some old-school manners. Nuance is hard in digital form. Do not assume Millennials know when or how to use please, thank you, or you're welcome. Remind Gen Xers and Boomers who've gotten sloppy in their communication that you expect common courtesies to be observed.

The Handwritten Thank-You Note

In this electronic age, nothing stands out more than a handwritten note on a nice card. Get yourself some nice stationery, perhaps personalized for added style, and take five minutes to handwrite a thank-you note. Take a moment to be specific in your thanks by calling attention to the action for which you are grateful.

Example:

> *Alice, thank you so much for your extra effort in the last week as we prepared for the new customer service platform. I appreciate your thoughtfulness and approach to the project, and think it will make a big difference to our customers.*
> *Best regards,*
> *John*

A note like the above means more than:

> *Alice—thanks for all your work.*
> *John*

If you need ideas on how to write different types of personal notes, pick up a copy of *101 Ways to Say Thank You* by Kelly Browne, *The Thank You Book* by Robyn Freedman Spizman, or another such guide.

If your handwriting is terrible, use an online service such as Bond (bondgifts.com) or Thank Goodness (thank-goodness.com) that lets you create your own stationery and dictate or type your note online and have it sent in real ink on a high-quality card.

The Pass-Along Thank-You

Don't forget to spread the love upward. The best part of my day is when I get an e-mail forwarded to me from an employee who gives a shout-out to someone else on the team for that person's contribution. I reply all—adding anyone else that makes sense—with an appropriate response; I use lots of capital letters and the exclamation point as a form of self expression, for example: AWESOME! Great Work! Great to hear. Thanks for all you do!

The pass-along e-mail:

- Shares kudos beyond the small group that knows about the work, informing other people of influence in the organization
- Allows the boss/leader to share in the appreciation, letting him not just acknowledge the person who did the work, but also the manager who shared the information
- Builds trust and appreciation for the manager—and an understanding that the manager realizes she is doing well because her people are doing well; it is critical that a manager not take credit for work done by teammates
- Reinforces that good work is appreciated

Group Appreciation at Team Meetings

Depending on the size of your company or team, you might meet once a week or once a month. Whatever your meeting schedule, it's important to reserve five minutes for appreciation, every single time. At Double Forte we do this several different ways:

Three Appreciations

Armed with the information that teams that visibly appreciate one another and give constructive feedback perform more effectively than those that don't, my company decided to end staff meetings with Three Appreciations. To do this, at the end of a meeting, everyone there randomly chooses three people to tell them, one by one, why they appreciate those people in the office or on the team. These expressions need to be sincere; they can be funny but should not be mundane. *Everyone*, including leadership, participates.

With everyone sharing their appreciations at the same time, it takes just five minutes and ends every meeting on a high note for everyone.

Just as different people have different preferences, different people bring different gifts to the team. Some are quiet observers, who, when they speak, can capture the whole room. Others are the class clowns who relieve tension with their offhand remarks. Do give relevant appreciations to the current situation and to the person you are speaking to. Be as specific as possible.

Examples of appreciative statements:

- I appreciate that you're always on time and prepared—it really helps the team out.
- I appreciate your positive attitude—it rubs off on everyone around you.
- I appreciate your curiosity—and that you're always bringing interesting and useful information to the group.
- I appreciate that you check in with me every day to see how I'm doing—I'm pretty shy, and your check-in really means a lot to me.
- I appreciate your leadership and that you're willing to answer any questions.
- I appreciate your communication style in the office—I'm trying to emulate that.

Avoid irrelevant appreciations, such as:

- I love your hair—I'm always trying to copy you.
- I love your shoes.

• I love watching you open the endless stream of boxes that get delivered here.

Practice this for four weeks. As one of my directors said to me, "Lee, I felt like a tool doing this the first two times, but now I get it." Lead the way in choosing a wide range of people to appreciate—not just your project teammates or direct reports. After it's not so uncomfortable, switch it up with other meeting send-offs, but keep it in the repertoire and insert it regularly.

Acrostic Memos Based on Team Members' Names

Get everyone on the team focused on recognizing the contributions of the rest of the team with acrostics. Susan Kramer, a director at my company, brought this technique to the team, and it's been incredibly positive and powerful.

An acrostic is a poem in which the first letter of each horizontal line spells out a word or phrase when read vertically. Usually, the first letter of each horizontal line is capitalized.

Write out every team member's name vertically on different pieces of paper. Pass out all the names, ensuring that no one gets his own. The presenter should give an example so everyone understands the exercise. Everyone then has twenty minutes to fill in the sheet, describing the person on the piece of paper with appreciations or observations. Because names vary in length, everyone who gets names with four letters or less, should add two words that come to mind about the person. After fifteen to twenty minutes, have everyone give his poem to the person named, who then posts it on his desk. It's an amazing thing to watch people's faces lighting up when they read their teammates' positive thoughts about them.

Example:

Affirmative Fold-Ups

Write the name of each team member on a different piece of paper and pass out the papers, being sure that no one gets her own name.

The first person writes an affirmative sentence at the bottom of the page and folds it up so that it can't be seen. The papers are then passed to the left, and the next person writes an affirmative sentence and folds the paper up again from the bottom. The papers keep getting passed until each person has five statements written about him. Distribute the pages to the "owners" and let them read the positive statements about their contribution or performance.

> Kindhearted
> Always smiling & positive
> Team player
> Intelligent
> Eager to learn & grow

Team Celebrations

Beyond celebrating individuals privately, find ways to celebrate people and teams in public to help create common understandings of people's achievements and/or life events.

- Celebrate personal work achievements, such as when work projects are completed well; recognize the person or team for their work.
- Applaud unexpected results. When someone does something beyond the call of duty, or displays work or effort

far above what you expect of her, it's time for the standing ovation. And when you present your colleague for the standing ovation, describe the work for which she is being recognized and explain to the rest of the team why it deserves the standing O.

- Break out the "Standing O Box." At my company, we created this unique method of acknowledging excellence: we purchased a supply of novelty boxes that, when opened, play a loud applause soundtrack. We affixed a "Standing O" logo to the top of the box, and personalized it with the recipient's name. Now, when people do good work throughout the day, people open up their boxes and we can hear the applause throughout the office. It makes us stop and ask what cool thing just happened. In the two years that we've given the standing O, each recipient has been surprised that we were talking about him. That it is usually unexpected is a wonderful thing – for the recipient and for the rest of the staff.

- Stand up and clap. Of course you don't need boxes with soundtracks to celebrate people's high achievements. Create your own live soundtrack by having everyone stand up and clap for the person or the team. Capture the moment with your camera phone and share it throughout the office.

When you plan your appreciation, recognize that each person on your team has her own preferences. Some will enjoy public accolades, while others will feel shy. While it's important to be consistent in how appreciation is delivered in public, it's equally important to not negate the accolades by making the recipient feel uncomfortable because of her individual style. For employees who are more reserved and do not want to be brought to the front of the room to receive their "award" or standing O or shout-out, deliver it to them wherever they are in the room, and then talk with that person later about your appreciation.

Appreciation Days

Create several appreciation days throughout the year to celebrate the contributions of those in certain roles, on particular teams, or support staff. Support staff, in particular, are often overlooked, but they are, by definition, the glue that keeps teams and companies running. Don't wait for the Hallmark holiday to surprise people with some heartfelt appreciation.

- Host a lunch in honor of the chosen role or of support staff. Create a poster for each person in the designated group and have the rest of the staff write appreciations on the poster. Present honorees with a funny hat, jacket, or T-shirt that represents what they mean to the office. Enlist a cross-section of team members to help create the celebration so you can capture the things you don't know about.
- Present a card that everyone has signed, cake, and gift certificates to support team members during a staff meeting.
- A few times a year send flowers to the receptionist and/or assistants, just because.

Celebrate and Honor Life Events

People come to work, people with families and friends in different conditions or stages in their lives—happy or sad, healthy or unhealthy. The more you can demonstrate your understanding of this, the more appreciated everyone—Millennials, Gen Xers, and Baby Boomers—will feel.

Celebrate or honor the significant milestones in people's lives throughout the year—birthdays, marriages, new children, recovery from major illnesses, and deaths in the family.

- Birthdays: consider lumping all birthdays in a month together and celebrating with cake and cards at a staff meeting or lunch.

- Marriages: hold a low-cost shower for the employee and let his or her fiancé join the festivities. Consider a cake, champagne, and a card. And it's a time for people who may not be invited to the wedding to chip in for a gift, which will be appreciated by the soon-to-be-wed and the rest of the team.
- New children, born into the family or adopted: the same type of celebration you organize for marriages is perfect for new additions to employees' families.
- Illness and/or deaths in the family: during emotional times, including illnesses and deaths in the family, it's important to check in with the employee and ask how you can support him. How far does this employee want the information to go? At the very least, a card of condolence is appropriate—if you coordinate a group card, add your own card as well. If you can, send flowers or donate to the charity of choice in your employee's name and let the person know you've made a donation.

  Small gestures mean a lot during difficult times like deaths and illnesses. If people on the staff want to jump in to help, keep them at bay until you know from the employee that he indeed wants the help. Do not assume everyone would like what you would like.
- Personal achievements: Give a public shout-out and/or send a note to people who meet personal goals, such as running a marathon, performing in a music group, completing extra courses, giving a speech at a local event, and so on.

Millennials are dinged often and loudly for wanting and expecting appreciation and acknowledgement for regular, run-of-the-mill things like showing up on time. In and of themselves, appreciation and acknowledgement are not bad. When used gratuitously, inauthentic appreciation and acknowledgement contribute to an individual's distorted view of his own contribution.

In contrast, when a business has an authentic culture of

appreciation and acknowledgement, that business performs better. Leadership's job is to redirect unproductive expectations and set guidelines and examples for what good behavior and appropriate celebrations are for everyone, not just the younger contingent.

Management Dos and Don'ts

- Do tell everyone that please and thank you do not mean that they are getting a promotion or a raise—rather, these are common courtesies.
- Do reinvigorate appreciation among your team with an intentional appreciation culture.
- Do teach people what you expect with regard to saying please and thank you, and teach them how to write e-mails that create good will and are constructive and polite.
- Don't assume everyone knows how to write a thank-you note.
- Do celebrate achievements.
- Do share other people's good work up the chain.
- Don't be shy about sharing appreciation.

Millennial Dos and Don'ts

- Do understand that a manager or colleague saying please and thank you to you does not mean you're getting a raise or a promotion.
- Don't assume please and thank you are just old school expressions and not needed.
- Do use please, thank you, and you're welcome with your peers in the office—out loud, in e-mails, in IM, and in text messages.
- Do share other people's good work up the chain.
- Do thank people for helping you and let their managers know that you are appreciative.

8

Give Clear Direction

The gap between intention and execution needs to be short and shallow.

—*Lee Caraher*

As you provide context and color that explain *why* all work is meaningful work, you will also need to provide direction for the result you seek and explain *how* the employee or team should get there. You'll also need to plan to give plenty of constructive and affirming feedback along the way. The result is the easiest piece of the puzzle: it's the easiest to say and it's also the easiest to assume that everyone understands. For that reason it's often skipped over: "Of course everyone knows what we're looking for in the finished product." No statement is more false.

Direction—The Goal

While it may seem counterintuitive, when we're articulating what we want the result to be—a document, a presentation, a meeting, a campaign—we have the perfect opportunity to solicit input and ideas from the team. "The goal is _____. How can we: Make it great? Minimize risk? Streamline it? Put something new into the mix?" You get the idea.

If you have examples from the past that serve as standards you'd like to maintain, share them. "Here's what we're looking for. Are there ways to improve this?"

By starting with the end in mind[1] and asking for input on how to maximize that end, we dramatically increase a person or a team's investment and buy-in, and we improve the odds that we'll get what we're looking for.

Direction—"How We Get There"

The "how we get there" part of the equation is harder to manage than the articulation of the goal. You probably have a good idea of how you'd like the different parts of the project done. Resist the urge to prescribe exactly how you think things should be done before soliciting input from the people who need to do the work.

Maybe no one will say anything and you'll get a blank stare when you ask, "How would you like to approach this?" Maybe you'll get a long, complicated answer that you think will send the person down several rabbit holes. Maybe you'll get exactly what you think should be done. Maybe you'll get a better idea than you've ever thought of. The important thing is that you've asked the question. Be open to whatever you get back.

- If you ask how you think the project should proceed and you get nothing, take a deep breath and say something like: "Okay, why don't you approach it this way, and the next time you might have some suggestions on how to improve the process."
- If you get what you think is a half-brained idea, look at it as an opportunity to coach the person through the project and relevant milestones. Use phrases like, "Let's take a look at that—how would that work?" or "Cool. How can we streamline that?" And then coach the employee to a productive way forward.
- If you get a better idea (be willing to hear that!), respond with "Great idea, let's set up some check-ins so we can make sure we stay on track."

Drive Out Ambiguity

Our business lexicon is full of ambiguity we don't recognize, maybe because older workers have a different understanding of the vocabulary.

While it might seem illogical setting deadlines is one of the most common places we find ambiguity in the workplace. Deadlines? Yes, deadlines. When is end of day? Or close of business? Or tomorrow? When is the end of the month? Later? Tuesday? *Never.* They are *never.* Whose day? Whose business? In what time zone? Until 11:59 p.m.? At 11:59 p.m. on the last day of the month, even if it's a Sunday? Tuesday—which one? And later never gets here...ever. As my mother used to say, "I said March; I didn't say which year."

You may feel you've given very clear deadlines that can't be misinterpreted, but unless you give a great deal of specificity, your team can disappoint you and be right...and nothing is more maddening.

In the end, the gap between intention and implementation needs to be short and shallow—and it's your job to describe your intentions with so much clarity that other people can implement to your expectations...the first time.

The Time Warp

One of the surprising elements I found in the interviews I conducted for this book concerned Millennials' different sense of time. "They have no sense of time," complained people under and over 34 years old.

Managers commented that Millennials "didn't spend enough time to do the job well," while Millennials consistently declared that they could "get the job done so much faster" than their managers. Here, dialogue and guidelines help everyone understand the changing work flows occurring today.

Managers, I encourage you to give estimated time required to finish the project well, and to add, "you may find a faster way to get this done. What I care about most is that the project is done well." Give a clear time guideline while acknowledging that the other person may know shortcuts that won't affect the quality of the work. Here's a great opportunity for managers to learn from younger colleagues. Many times I've learned shortcuts that didn't impact the quality of the work that my younger colleagues applied once they tackled the task.

The discussion about the time frame of the work also provides a forum for feedback if what comes back does not fit the bill. If that's what happens, you can probe how the employee approached the work and pinpoint where shortcuts were taken without an appreciation for how they might impact the quality of the work. In the dialogue you have you'll be able to reinforce the quality message and discuss what shortcuts or workarounds can be made that don't impact the final product—you may even learn a new way to cut thirty minutes from your own work flow.

Millennials, I urge you to listen to the guidelines and follow them...at least the first time. Once you complete an assignment as it's been outlined by your manager, you'll be able to see the whole picture. *Then* you'll be able to improve on it and get the same or a better result, and your way will have a better chance of being appreciated and adopted.

Deadline Specificity

When giving deadlines, be specific: provide exact times on exact dates.

Examples:

Replace: EOD or end of day	with	5 p.m., Tuesday, February 2
Replace: COB or close of business	with	6:30 p.m., Wednesday, March 3
Replace: later	with	4 p.m. today

Replace: end of month	with	Friday, March 29, at 2 p.m.
Replace: Tuesday	with	Tuesday, September 3, at 10 a.m.
Replace: tomorrow	with	Tomorrow, Thursday, at 3 p.m.
Replace: come see me soon	with	Please get on my calendar before next Friday at 3

This level of granularity can't be misconstrued. If you provide this type of specificity and your employee or team misses deadlines, it's not a matter of misunderstood expectations.

Formats and Condition/Status

"I never would have dreamed of sending an unfinished product to my boss," says Dan, forty-five. "And now all I ever get are half-assed efforts that I need to totally rewrite to get them done—it'd be faster and easier for me to do the work myself."

It's not enough to say, "Please send me the report by Tuesday, September 3 at 10 a.m."

In interview after interview, managers across the country in different industries described getting work product with loose outlines instead of fully formed ideas, reports, or recommendations ready for distribution. They also complained that they were submitted drafts that were full of inaccuracies, typos, or messy language.

"When I tell people that their work isn't done I often get, 'You didn't say you wanted it to be final' or 'I thought you would just fix any problems.' How is this even a possibility?" says Michelle, forty-three.

It may seem incredible, but in order to get what you want, you need to articulate exactly what you want in your instructions. Always. Do not assume that the other person knows what you mean or holds the same expectation of delivery that you do. Ambiguity is in the eye of the beholder. As long as someone else can say, "I thought you meant" or "I didn't know that" and be right, you are rolling the dice on the work submitted to you.

Replace:

Replace: send me your ideas	with	Please send me a short (no more than four-paragraph) e-mail with your ideas on how to approach this project
Replace: send me the report	with	Please send me the report as close to final as you can make it, in report format, and ready to be passed along to Sally
Replace: send me a draft	with	Please send me what you feel is a final draft Consider adding: check last year's report for formatting and content standards
Replace: let me know your thoughts	with	I'd like to see your thoughts about the report and the implications it has for our project; send these together with an outline of how you think we should proceed in an e-mail

Revisions

If you get work full of typos and loose language, send it back and tell the person it's not ready to be reviewed.

Here's a sample response:

Hi Tim,

You must have sent me the wrong version. Please take a look and make sure that the report [e-mail/memo] is typo free, is in the standard format, uses tight, active language, and is something that I can pass along to Sally. Please send this to me by tomorrow, Tuesday, at 10 a.m.

   Thanks,
   Peter

If this has happened before, respond with something like:

Hi Tim,

This version is not ready for me to review. Please take a look and make sure you've got all of the information you need and that the document is correctly formatted, free of typos, and uses active language and concise sentence structure. I expect this back to me by tomorrow, Tuesday, at 10 a.m.

   Thanks,
   Peter

And a third time (please, no):

Hi Tim,

This is not ready for me to review. Please take a look at my last e-mail and make sure you follow all of the direction there. Please see me by 5 p.m. today to check in on your status.

   Thanks,
   Peter

Or

Hi Tim,

This is not ready for me to review. Please come see me at 10 a.m. today to discuss how you're going to get this finished by 5 p.m. today.

Thanks,

Peter

Quality

Another common complaint about the way Millennials work concerns the quality of the thinking or work process. "They think the first answer they find with a simple Google search is the answer and sufficient to base a recommendation on," says Nancy, fifty. Or, as Perry, fifty-two, adds, "They just want to get things off their list so they can move onto the next thing. They don't seem to care whether it's done right or well."

First of all, we all know that less-than-quality work is *not* the hallmark of Millennials alone—it's common to people from all generations who either (A) don't know what quality is or (B) don't care what quality is. Until you've proved that A is not true, don't move onto B. Schooled to ace the test and not necessarily master the material, Millennials may never have been shown or taught how to vet sources and assemble an informed point of view from a variety of good sources.

While I love Googling as much as the next person, the phrase "Just Google it" is as grating as fingernails on a chalkboard to me. We can prove over and over again that where the first link takes us or what is on the first page of any search result is most likely not enough to create a well-informed understanding of a subject (unless, perhaps, the search is on Justin Bieber).

For anyone new to your organization or team, it's important to set the tone and provide guidelines for the quality of work you expect before they start. Don't waste time—yours or theirs—assuming they will know what you expect. Spend ten minutes before someone starts on a project to *describe* the quality of the work you expect if you want to raise your odds of *receiving* the quality of work you expect.

While it may seem obvious to you, one person's full analysis is another person's snapshot. Be as specific as possible.

For example:

- Identify any sources you want to make sure are included.
- How would you characterize the work—in-depth? Top-line? Snapshot?
- Do you need to have a certain number of sources? Top one hundred? Ten?
- Do you have an example of good previous work you can share to give context?

Replace—"I need a full analysis of last quarter's sales" with "I need a full analysis of last quarter's sales by customer, salesperson, product, and price point. Please take a look at the last two quarters as a comparison and identify any trends. I'll look forward to your assessment of any opportunities you think we have. I think this may take four hours."

And once your employee gets it, you can say, "Great job last time, can you please do the same thing and bring any learnings forward this month?"

Use E-mail to Your Advantage

E-mail is hell. It's a hell of redundant messages, most of which are required to get the point across because the originator did not provide enough context, specificity, or instructions in the first e-mail.

The point of communication is to deliver a concept that can be well understood by the recipient. We've all gotten lazy with e-mail. Based on e-mail patterns in my inbox, I believe we can reduce e-mail volume by more than 55 percent if we drive ambiguity out of e-mail.

To wit:

To: Quail Team
From: Lee
Re: Meeting on Caller Project Progress
Date: Monday, June 2, 2012 3:14 p.m.

Quail team,
I'd like to meet for a progress check-in on the Caller Project next week. Please let me know where you're available next week for forty-five minutes.
Thanks,
Lee

To: Lee
From: Joe
Cc: Quail Team
RE: RE: Meeting on Caller Project Progress
Date: Monday, June 2, 2012 3:15 p.m.

Lee,
I'm available anytime on Wednesday or Thursday. Do you want everyone to report on his or her responsibilities or a topline? Do you want a PowerPoint? Who should drive that? What do you want to see before the meeting?
Thanks,
Joe

To: Lee
From: Liam
Cc: Quail Team
RE: RE: Meeting on Caller Project Progress
Date: Monday, June 2, 2012 3:16 p.m.

Lee,
I can meet on Thursday. Do you want the whole team there? I'm not sure everyone is here next week. What

format? Any key metrics you're looking for? What's the
outcome you're looking for?
 Thanks,
 Liam

And so on.

It's enough to send you into a fetal position under your desk once your hand's been wrapped in a cast for carpal tunnel syndrome due to so much unnecessary typing.

To avoid unnecessary back-and-forth, drive as much clarity as possible into the first e-mail. Provide context, name exactly who is responsible for what, give deadlines, and provide opportunity for the team to bring to your attention items you haven't considered or heard about. If you're using a global e-mail list, call out specific people who have action items—don't assume people will know they're supposed to do anything.

To: Joe; Sally
Cc: Quail Team
From: Lee
Re: Meeting on Caller Project Progress
Date: Monday, June 2, 2012 3:14 p.m.

Quail team,
 I'd like to meet for a progress check-in on the Caller Project next week either Wednesday at 2 or Thursday at 10—Jane will confirm with you.
 Joe and Sally, please take the lead on this with input from the rest of the team. I'd like to see overall status of the project elements with special attention to the Community Plan and Packaging. If there are any other elements that are in yellow or red, please bring those forward as well. Anything on schedule without issues need not be discussed during the meeting. PowerPoint

will be best. I'd like to see the report by 6 p.m. the night
before—Jane will confirm deadline with you.
   Thanks,
   Lee

While e-mail is great for keeping track of (sometimes inane) conversations, we get lazy quickly in our effort to plow through it all. And in that laziness we increase the chance of details being lost—important details such as deadlines, formats, or other requirements.

Drive ambiguity out of your e-mail strings by striking the following from your e-mail vocabulary: Start reading at the bottom. Never start an e-mail with "Read from the bottom"—you are just inviting confusion. Bring all of the key facts forward in your reply so that in one screen everyone can see the scope, deadlines, context, and responsibilities.

E-Mail Dos and Don'ts:

- Do provide as much of the desired result as possible in your e-mail: deadlines, responsibilities, and context.
- Do name specific people's tasks if you're using a global list, so that person knows he has something to do.
- Don't assume everyone will be able to keep track of all of the details in a long e-mail string.
- Do bring the details to the top of an e-mail string.
- Don't require people to "start at the bottom" to get all the details, deadlines, and requirements.

Clarify Assumptions from the Start

Whoever said assumptions make an "ass out of U and me" was a genius. A true genius. For management and Millennials alike, assumptions about an event, project, or rule often mean that the two groups end up on polar ends of the spectrum of understanding.

Management: "I assumed they knew what I was talking about."

Millennial: "I assume they will help me do the job"

Management: "I assume they know what is expected."

Millennial: "I assume they will tell me what they want and will give me the tools to do it."

Management: "I assume everyone just needs to do their job."

Millennials: "I assume you'll tell me how my job fits in with the rest of the teams'."

Lots of assumptions. And too often we learn that our assumptions diverged before the project even started, though we didn't realize that until after we'd executed a plan to less than satisfactory results.

Why does this happen? Because we don't voice our assumptions. We all need to get better at thinking about and articulating our assumptions before we start our work. In chapter 4 I talked about how important context is for Millennials—and the rest of us—to effectively engage in the work at hand. A big part of context are assumptions—those factors we take for granted as fact or commonly held (yet unarticulated) beliefs. Beyond the purpose of the project and individual roles in it, take the time to articulate your assumptions and solicit your team members' assumptions as well.

For example:

1. How long do you expect the work to take?
2. What do you expect people to do if they hit a roadblock?
3. What is the desired outcome? How should it look?
4. What are the check ins?
5. When do you need to have people in the office? By when?

And so on.

What does your team expect? Ask them!

1. What do you think you need to succeed?
2. What do you think the outcome will be?
3. What kind of impact can we make?
4. What's the competition going to do?

And so on.

What happens when things go awry? Too often if we actually take the time to review a project—what went well and what did not, we ignore assumptions that each team member carried into the assignment. And by ignoring them you're stacking the deck against making the kind of exponential difference you want to make the next time you try.

A good step to take when examining a work plan's results or process breakdown is to examine the results you got, examine how closely you adhered to the plan (what got in the way or changed) then adjust the plan based only on what happened. If your team does this single-loop process Plan-Do-Adjust, you will be ahead of most teams, but chances are high that you will only be incrementalizing your way forward.

Single-Loop Learning

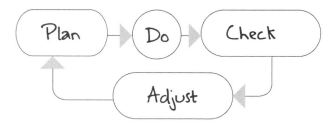

With Single-Loop learning,[2] there's a real danger of repeating ourselves without getting to the root of why we're disappointed with the results or the process. A better, no great, step to actually fundamentally improving outcomes and processes is to incorporate Double-Loop learning when examining project results. Double-Loop learning puts into the process the step that allows us to align on the assumptions we held going into the project: assumptions about the market and the competition, as well as the assumptions about who's going to do what, deadlines and dependencies.

Double-Loop Learning

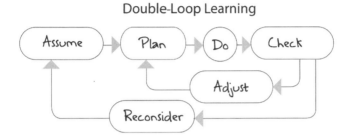

By articulating assumptions at the beginning, you will drive ambiguity out *at the start* of a project. By looping back to the assumptions, not just adjusting the plan, after completing a project, you will be able to plan better for ongoing work.

This is how teams get better together, become more efficient, and get better results: by aligning their assumptions, driving out ambiguity, and continually revisiting the assumptions to ensure that everyone's pulling the oars in the same direction. And when your team includes people from different generations, double-loop learning gets everyone on the same page quickly and without ambiguity.

Checking back in with the team on process and improvements is not a sign of weakness or pandering. It is the hallmark of good leadership. By consistently driving double-loop learning into the project management, to continually reaffirm or challenge the assumptions everyone is working from, everyone can learn how to drive efficiency into group dynamics.

By being as clear as possible in your direction, you are setting an example for how thoroughly you want your team to work and how the team members can support one other in their interdependent work.

Give Direction Early and Often

I work in San Francisco, a city that attracts people from all over the world. We come together, with our different cultures and different upbringings, and bring our different perspectives together. No wonder we have issues "standardizing" expectations of behavior. And this is true throughout the country— people I talked with in the Northeast, Northwest, Midwest, South, and Southwest all talked about the same phenomenon.

So how can we get everyone on the same page without feeling like micromanagers? Start early, repeat often, and find fun ways to reinforce standards.

Onboarding is the first in-depth opportunity you have to convey your expectations. During the onboarding process, it's critical that new employees understand their own role, their team's purpose, and how they and the team fit into the company's vision and mission, but it's also crucial that they understand the cultural and practical expectations of how a team or company works.

Some of the key questions/topics you should start clarifying from day one are outlined here. As you will see there are many different ways to answer these standard questions – the more clarity you can drive into the answers, the better off you will be setting clear expectations for everyone from the beginning.

What are your expectations for office hours? Choose what makes sense for you.

- Everyone has the same hours?
- Normal arrival time is between 7:30 and 9 a.m., and if you're going to be later than that you need to let your team know. OR
- Normal arrival is by 10 a.m., and departure by 9 p.m.

- You can work from home when it works for the team, but remote work needs to be approved beforehand. OR
- You can work from home whenever you like. OR
- You can't work from home.
- Doctor and dental appointments can be scheduled throughout the day, but you need to ask if the schedule works for the team and the work at hand. If not, you need to reschedule unless it's an emergency.

How do you approach conference calls and meetings?

- Arrive five minutes early.
- Always have an agenda.
- If people on the team are in different places for a call and the team is talking with someone outside the organization, everyone is on IM, so you can coordinate answers.
- Never leave a meeting or conference call without clearly defined next steps.
- Always send an e-mail/memo summarizing the decisions made and next steps.
- Everyone goes to every meeting. OR
- You may not attend everything—the team leader will decide if you attend or not.
- Leave cell phones off or muted.
- Don't look at cell phones or e-mail during meetings or calls.

What are office norms?

- If you're sick we expect you to stay home. AND
- If you're sick, please notify your manager and the office manager as soon as possible by e-mail.
- Everyone takes their dishes to the kitchen and puts them in the dishwasher. OR
- No one leaves dirty plates at their desk. OR

- The office manager will come by and pick up your dirty dishes.
- Staff meetings are attended by all, so no scheduling outside meetings during staff meetings, unless the matter is urgent.
- Use your office phone for company calls and personal calls that aren't too personal. OR
- Take your personal calls behind closed doors—what's personal is personal.
- Don't leave your medication out for everyone to see.

Is there a dress code?

- You may wear whatever you want as long as it's clean and covers your privates. OR
- We are business casual—that means jeans are welcome as long as they don't have holes, frays, or are cut/hang so low that your underwear or tattoo shows (no matter how cool that is). Yes, I know those jeans are your most expensive ones. Yes, I know you spent painstaking hours distressing them perfectly. No, they're still not okay. OR
- We dress in business attire at the office. That means suits and ties for men, and suits or professional coordinates for women.
- No open-toed shoes. OR
- Any clean shoes except flip flops or Lucite stilettos.
- Casual Friday—no jeans. OR
- Casual Friday—jeans allowed.
- No bare midriffs or exposed backs.
- Tattoos are okay except on the face. OR
- Cover all tattoos.
- No skirts shorter than two inches above the knee. Or four inches above the knee.
- No perfume.

The company dress code should not be a surprise to a new employee. This should be covered in the recruiting process.

What are the expectations for dinner with the big cheese, a client, or another external partner?

- Seating will be specified by the team leader.
- Put your napkin in your lap when you sit down.
- Silence your phone and don't look at or answer it at the table.
- Don't have more than two drinks. OR
- Have one drink less than our guests or the boss.
- Wait for everyone to be served before you start eating.
- The team leader will pick up the check.
- Do not brush your hair or apply lipstick at the table.

My Experience: Train What You Can

Dining out is a minefield with your team members unless you're sure they know what you expect. I used to make lunch out part of our recruiting process, until we had passed on two great candidates because they didn't know how to eat at a restaurant. Then I realized that they could be taught what's expected once they were in the company.

What is the office e-mail etiquette?

- Always use a subject header.
- Always spell check before you send.
- Turn on send delay to five minutes so you can retrieve something if you need to.
- People who have something to do go in the "To" line; everyone else goes into the "cc" line.
- Reply to all e-mail within two hours. Four hours. Twenty-four hours. (Everyone needs this type of guideline, with

whatever time frame makes sense for the organization—
truly, everyone does.)

- If you're not in the "To:" line, don't reply unless you have
  pertinent information that will help the person or people
  in the "To:" line.
- Turn on your auto-reply out-of-office message if you're
  going to be out for more than four hours. OR
- Never turn on your auto-reply message.

Reinforcing Expectations

At my company, we found that everyone had a different definition of business casual and a different understanding of dining
etiquette, as well as varying expectations about other conduct.
We began covering these topics in the onboarding process, but
found that people benefited from being reminded from time to
time.

Games

To reinforce expectations, consider putting the company's
expectations about conduct into a game show format à la
Jeopardy or *Family Feud*.

Etiquette *Jeopardy*. Fill a wall with your team's etiquette
guidelines, grouping them under different categories. Divide
the group into teams; use an Eggspert buzzer to let people
buzz in to answer questions.

> **Player:** "I'll take Conference Calls for two hundred."
> **Moderator:** "The answer is five minutes."
> **First player to buzz:** "What is 'How many minutes early
> should we dial into a conference call'?"

Etiquette *Family Feud*. Divide the team into two sides. Rank
the guidelines by priority of importance, and assign numerical

value so that total number of priority points is one hundred (for example: "Call in five minutes early" is twenty-four points, "Always have an agenda" is twenty, "Turn off cell phones" is nineteen, etc.) Use an Eggspert buzzer to let people buzz in.

> **Moderator:** Name something that is important for conference calls.
> **First player to buzz:** Always have an agenda
> **Moderator says:** Let's see "Have an agenda!" Survey says, twenty!

The winning team gets lunch or drinks or some other fun reward. It's dorky, but fun, and it gets everyone involved. Everyone gets some reinforcement out of this kind of game, and you've had some fun to boot.

Reference Guides

While I think it's true that everyone could benefit from a quarterly browse through Emily Post's *The Etiquette Advantage in Business,*[3] that three-inch-thick hardback book is cumbersome and expensive to put on everyone's desk—and it's bound to get put out of sight, never to see the light of day. If you happen to have a copy, browse it every once in a while. (Tip: It's a great gift for college students. They may look at you askance, but it'll be well worth the rolled eyes.)

Staff Reminders

Once every two months or so, choose one business etiquette topic and review the guidelines for that topic at your staff meeting. It'll take five minutes and serve as a good reminder for everyone.

Every two months or so, send an e-mail reviewing the guidelines or clarifying any misapprehensions that may have arisen.

1. **EverythingSpeaks Desktop Guide.** To make it easier to keep manners top of mind after orientation, I created EverythingSpeaks, a desktop guide to manners. It's a Lucite box of colorful cards that sits on people's desks. Each card has a different piece of office protocol, written with humor (I hope) and featuring an illustration that helps make the point. Categories include: first impressions, conference calls, dining out, and so on. This way we can just pull a card for a category we want to reinforce and use them as reminders without being intimidating or preachy.

It's a lot to cover, but all guidelines for expected conduct need to be described, and in some detail. Don't let people's inappropriate behavior make you crazy and build bad impressions of themselves or your company when they probably just don't know better—really, they probably don't know better.

Management Dos and Don'ts

- Do provide exact times, dates, and required formats or guidelines when giving deadlines.
- Do be explicit and reiterate expectations.
- Don't use ambiguous terms such "end of day" "close of business" or "later" when giving deadlines.
- Do give time estimates for work, but be open to hearing about ways to do the tasks faster.
- Don't accept work that is not completed to your satisfaction; give it back with clear instruction.
- Do tell your employee it's good work when it is good work
- Do articulate your assumptions to the whole team before a project starts.
- Do ask what everyone's assumptions and expectations are—regarding their own work and that of others—before you start a project.
- Do make sure that everyone understands how her work impacts the rest of the team's.

Millennial Dos and Don'ts

- Do ask for clarification when you don't have specific instruction.
- Don't start until you know what's expected from you.
- Do ask for specific deadlines so that you know exactly when something is due.
- Do ask how long things should take; if you're done early review the instructions one more time to make sure you have completed the project (run spell check!).
- Do ask for sample work to use as a guideline.
- Do show your older colleagues how you shaved time off the project—they will appreciate it!
- Do things your manager's way first—and then improve it
- Do let people know if you're not getting the expected results as soon as you know so the team can revisit assumptions with this new data.

9

Feedback Is a Gift

Feedback is a gift.
—*Lee Caraher*

Why does this group need so much feedback?" asks Susan, a fifty-five-year-old hedge fund manager. "We hire the best of the best, and I still can't believe how much feedback the under-thirties need."

Feedback, the need and the desire for it, emerges consistently as a theme with and for Millennials. On the one hand, managers bemoan that they are constantly interrupted with requests for off-schedule check-ins to "make sure I'm on the right track." On the other hand, managers expressed incredulity that their younger colleagues are so clueless. "Why don't they know?" was a constant refrain in almost every conversation.

I'm going to guess that every Baby Boomer's and GenXer's boss said this about him sometime in the early part of his career. It's like the pushmi-pullyu from the Doctor Dolittle stories—there exists a tension between what people ask for and what they really need, leaving managers stranded between being helpful and being perceived as a micromanager. It's enough to send us running for the bottle. The best gift we can give our colleagues *all year long* is corrective and redirecting feedback in a way that can be heard to help them capitalize on the great things they're doing and to improve on those skills on their growing edges. This is a gift that costs nothing, and when given, saves time and reduces frustration all around. In the end, feedback is a gift we give ourselves.

Not that feedback is easy to give, or to hear, at first. Like all good things, giving and receiving redirecting feedback requires practice.

Timing counts heavily in effective feedback. The key is to correct people as close as possible to the moment that it's needed. When weeks or months pass, it can feel to the employee that the incident is ancient history dredged up to find fault. It's also important to give feedback in a timely manner so that your frustration does not fester and grow. Tell people how they can improve as soon as you see that they need it, so that employees don't keep on going without knowing they aren't performing to your expectations, expectations they may not understand.

Daphne, executive director of a nationally known think tank, avoided telling her young associate that he couldn't just decide to stroll in at 10 a.m. because, she says, "I didn't want to seem bitchy and I figured he'd catch on after he saw that he was always the last one in the office." She was ultimately faced with telling her younger colleague that the previous six months had not been satisfactory. She knew to expect some backlash from the young man, and indeed got it: "He said it was unfair to go so long without telling him that he was doing something that could hurt his performance review. He was right."

They cleared the air and have moved forward with much clearer expectations of what they expect from each other. Now Daphne is trying "much harder to address things when they come up" instead of assuming that people will just notice and do the right thing.

My Own Process: A 360 Review

In 2013 I asked my business coach, Lori Ogden Moore, to conduct a 360 review for me. This requires a bit of a different process, because I'm the boss and really report to no one, or to everyone, depending on how you look at it.

We asked my direct reports, colleagues on nonprofit boards on which I'm a director, and clients who know me best to evaluate my performance on a spectrum of criteria in the Leadership Circle[1] model.

I was a bit (okay, more than a bit) wary. The last time I'd had a 360, the results spun me into depression when I realized that, while my superiors and my direct and indirect reports scored me very high, my colleagues did not. In fact, I scored lowest in the entire forty-plus-person cohort of executive and senior vice presidents in the worldwide agency. But leadership of your own company can put you in a bubble of "yes," and leaders get no feedback on how they can improve. So into the depths of the 360 I went—voluntarily, mind you.

My 360 was the biggest gift I got last year (apologies to my husband, who rocks it in the gift department)—and it continues to be the gift that keeps on giving. Here, on a single chart, I can see where I should double down, where I can lighten up, and where I can keep on keepin' on. Only with honest input can I make adjustments in my language, behavior, or habits and become a better leader. I'm very thankful for all the people who participated in my anonymous survey—the feedback has been so very helpful.

Feedback People Need

Giving feedback is challenging for everyone. I take that back. Giving feedback that people can actually hear, absorb, and act on is challenging for everyone. It is so challenging that many managers and leaders avoid giving it, preferring to sidestep what could turn into a conflict or confrontation.

No one wants to keep doing things the wrong way. I believe everyone wants the feedback they need to be effective in their jobs. They want it even if it's embarrassing. They want you to help them be their best. Most of all, they want input and correction delivered in a way that is respectful—a way that honors their effort to date, while offering a better, more fruitful way forward.

In *Leadership and the Art of Conversation*,[2] which I encourage everyone to read, Kim H. Krisco explores effective ways to use conversation and language as a management tool, so people can hear and apply feedback. "If managers change the way they talk to people," explains Krisco, "they can become much more effective managers—they can become great leaders."[3]

Using Effective Language

The challenge with feedback is not only giving it, but also having it be heard. There are two language changes you can make right now to be more effective.

Strike Why Questions from Your Repertoire

Even if you don't mean them to, "Why?" questions sound accusatory and judgmental more often than they sound open and inquisitive. With "Why?" most people hear "You're stupid."

- "*Why* did you do it that way?"
- "*Why* would you say that?"
- "*Why* are we talking about this?"

You may intend an open dialogue but you've set up a defensive one with the Why? question. Instead, open the conversation with affirmations first and then ask "How?" or "What?" questions that get to the matter at hand.

- "Good effort. How should we go forward?"
- "I know we had great expectations. What do you think happened? How will we avoid this in the future?"

- "That's interesting. What do you suggest as a next step?"
- "Tell me more about what informed this decision. Let's figure this out together."

This has been the most challenging change I've tried to make in my own leadership language. I'd say I'm successful about half the time. But now, as soon as "Why?" comes out of my mouth, I'm able to adjust and reframe the question so that the person or people I'm talking with don't immediately go on the defensive.

The Power of "And"

As Bill Gross, founder and CEO of Idealab, says, "When you start telling someone, 'You are really great at X, but' the *but* negates all the goodwill that you are building up with the first part of your sentence. The *but* gets someone's defenses up, and makes them way less able to hear the important thing you want them to listen to."[4]

Use "and" instead of "but," and you can be much more successful in helping the other person hear you and achieve the goal. To do this, write out the "but" clause you'd like to use and then find a new way to get your point across with an "and" clause.

For example:

Go from: "Jean, you are great at project management, *but* you need to make sure you don't laugh at people who don't understand the task at hand."

To: "Jean, you are great at project management, *and* you'd be even more effective if you would take the time to explain the task at hand to the people who don't get it the first time."

Of course, this is not Millennial-exclusive advice. This is language you should use with everyone. Although, if you're predisposed to think Millennials only want positive feedback and can't hear constructive criticism, really take this to heart.

Feedback People Ask For

Millennials get dinged for asking for feedback all the time and "then not being able to take it," as Leo, forty-eight, says. "They don't know how to take criticism—why do they ask for feedback if they don't want to hear how to improve something?"

The conundrum of feedback is that there's a disconnect between employees expecting affirming feedback and needing constructive criticism. And, of course, the way different people deliver criticism, no matter how well intentioned, can contribute to employees feeling hurt or misunderstanding the point of the critique.

> ### Boomer Insight: Mike, age fifty-seven
>
> "They need to learn to take criticism. This isn't the little league baseball team, where everyone is a winner. You need to work hard and gain respect from your supervisors. They are not automatically going to think you're great. Your attitude, and an expressed desire to learn from criticism, is important to getting ahead."

"I had a woman on my staff who was constantly lurking by my office to get my attention. She'd wait during meetings or when I was on the phone. And even though we had a time to check in, she couldn't wait because she 'didn't want to waste her time' if I didn't like what she was doing. It drove me crazy," shares Elizabeth, fifty-two, about one of her younger colleagues. When I asked Elizabeth what she had said to her colleague to discourage this behavior she was silent, and then admitted, "Nothing." Here's the deal. It's on you if you're frustrated with behavior that you haven't addressed with people.

Milestone Setting

When employees ask for feedback at too-frequent or inconveniently timed intervals, we need to work at weaning them from input given throughout the process and focus them on getting feedback at predetermined milestones.

We need to build in check-ins that allow enough time to fix things if the work is not ready for prime time. And we also need to transfer the work fully to our team members so that they start carrying the full load of their responsibility.

And it is a weaning process for some. That sounds maternal, I know. I don't know a better word to describe the process. We need to meet our staff where they are, not expect them to leap beyond what they know without guidance. If we help our colleagues on their journey to where they want to go, they will be more valuable contributors to the organization and less irritating for you.

The Tough Conversations

For a variety of reasons, most people I talked with don't like to have the hard conversations with their colleagues, partners, or clients. Some people simply hate confrontation, while others don't want to be "the heavy," and still others don't want to put the time or effort into hard conversations because they believe they are a waste of time, and that the employees won't change.

Good teams—those with a variety of like-minded and diverse points of view—address and resolve issues for everyone's clarification and benefit. Good teams find a good, interdependent way forward after conflict and keep working on any issues over time. While I don't think most people intend to cause conflict or frustration, it happens. We are all human.

Participating on teams effectively is hard work, and good teams should be protected at all costs; learning how to handle conflict effectively is a key skill each team member, of any age, needs to master.

Among the many excellent tools we use at my company is the communication circle, which executive coaches Lori Ogden Moore and Susi Watson adapted based on work done at Georgetown University. By working through the communication circle, people separate facts, feelings, reasons, and blame, and are able to articulate specific requests to rectify a situation and explain how they can help the team work well. Using the communication circle also allows people to put some time between the incident that broke their frustration threshold and the conversation about it, so that they're more equipped to reach a productive solution.

When the ship's going down is not the time to ask why the hell someone drove into the iceberg. When there's time to impact the outcome or after a disappointing result or event is the time to ask for a meeting to discuss what is happening or happened and how to fix it going forward.

Figure based on work done at Georgetown University by Lori Ogden Moore and Susi Watson.

The communication circle is a simple process that helps break down the parts of conflict to get to a productive collaborative agreement about how to proceed. Before the meeting, one or both of the people fill out the circle with their facts, assessments, feelings, requests, and offers. Usually the person calling the meeting goes first, walking the other person through their circle. Then the other person has a chance to respond to the assessments, requests, and offers and/or goes through their own circle. Together the two (or more) people agree on a way forward in the spirit of improving outcomes, processes and/or team dynamics.

Step 1—Facts: Start with the facts on which everyone can agree.

"The document was late."

Step 2—Assessment: Articulate your assessment of why these facts are true.

"My assessment is that you waited to start the work until the deadline was near, underestimated how long it would take, and got stuck balancing it with the rest of your work."

Step 3—Feelings: State your feelings about the situation. Do *not* skip this step! Feelings are important so that people can better understand your point of view.

"I feel angry that you left me hanging and I had to stay late to make sure the document was completed on time so it could be included in the report to the board."

Step 4—Request: Make the request that will prevent the fact from happening again.

"My request is that you deliver this document a day earlier next month, and that you let me know at least two hours ahead of time if it looks like you're not going to be able to make the deadline. That way, I can help you or reprioritize your workload so you can get this important document done."

Step 5—Offer: Make an offer to the other person of how you can help him avoid the situation in the future.

"My offer to you is to check in with you first thing on the deadline day to make sure you have everything you need to get the document done."

Finally, the other person responds to the assessment, request, and offer with agreements or alterations and/or goes through their own circle. The point is that both sides are heard and can use these steps to air grievances and solve problems together.

By walking through issues with these five steps, anyone can address an issue that is squelching performance, sowing ill will, or causing conflict among even the best of teams. Every team is going to have issues. Good teams resolve them quickly.

Generous Feedback Is a Cultural Thing

Feedback does not belong solely to the realm of management—everyone, no matter what her title or role, can provide constructive feedback. "Great job! I like the way you wrote the recommendation." Or, "Good stuff. So that you know, you swayed a bit while you were talking. Next time, try planting your left foot a bit in front of your right foot." Or, "I really liked what you had to say. So that you know, you slid into up-talking a bit, which made it a little harder to hear." And one of my colleagues was brave enough to say to me, "Lee, when your eyes bug out it looks like you're really mad." (I'm usually not, I'm usually just thinking hard.)

The worst thing we can do to our colleagues is to let them swim in ignorance. Giving feedback—positive and negative—in a constructive manner that can be heard is the ultimate gift to your colleagues, and one that generates reciprocity.

My Own Story: Embarrassing Feedback

Early in my career—I was twenty-seven—I had one of the most embarrassing feedback sessions a person could have. I had risen quickly in the organization and was set for another promotion. It was a promotion that would not come, however, until I corrected one thing: my appearance. When I look back on it, I can see what my boss and project managers were trying to tell me by dropping hints, though I did not recognize them as such—and I'm usually a quick study. Finally, Malinda, one of my bosses took me to lunch and told me, in the nicest way possible, that my appearance— my clothing and my hair—was getting in my way. Clearly, management had talked about me at length, and not about my work, but about how I looked. I was mortified. But even with my embarrassment, I was willing to hear suggestions to remedy the situation. Within two weeks I had the beginnings of a new wardrobe and was on the way to presentable hair. A month later, management set me on the path of helping everyone else—four people—they had identified as needing help in the appearance department. I still get a funny feeling in my stomach when I tell the story, even though the feedback was what I needed to hear.

Management Dos and Don'ts

- Do articulate your expectations for behavior, standards, and dress early on and remind people.
- Don't sound preachy.
- Do remove "but" clauses and "Why?" questions from your vocabulary.
- Don't assume your people were raised the same way you were and inherently know what is expected of them.

- Do give feedback in a timely manner.
- Don't hold feedback until you can't take it anymore.
- Do use the communication circle to help resolve issues between people or among groups.
- Do find fun ways to reinforce your expectations.

Millennials Dos and Don'ts

- Do ask what is expected of you.
- Do be open to some rules that may be new to you.
- Do pay attention to how experienced people in the group dress, address e-mails, and present themselves in meetings, and adopt their norms.
- Don't stick out for the wrong reasons.
- Do ask, not tell, your manager before you work from home or leave early for a doctor's appointment.
- Don't say, "That's too early for me" when you're asked to show up early for an important meeting or workday.

10

Be Transparent

We can see you.

—*Ben, age twenty-eight*

Transparency builds trust, loyalty, and ambassadorship. Transparency builds a level of employee engagement that money, even lots of it, cannot buy. Telling people, of all ages and levels, what you can share about the business is vital if you want to keep people focused, efficient, and productive. The telephone game has sped up, and today misinformation can travel and snowball faster than at any time in history.

"Management providing transparency is really important," says Andrew, twenty-six, associate on Wall Street. "Information is readily available—we know how to get the information we want." Business today needs to be prepared to be as "open a book as possible so that rumors don't get out of hand," explains Joe, thirty-nine. "My parents were stoic, both at home and at work. I think that style doesn't fly for these Millennial staffers."

Communicate All The News You Can

Communicate when things are going well and when they aren't going as well as you'd like them to. Resist the urge to gloss over difficult situations by saying things like, "Everything is fine, the business is doing great" when they aren't and it isn't. Millennials, and the rest of us, want to be in on the truth; all employees want to know that leadership respects them enough and trusts them enough to tell them the truth. Your team can help more when they know what is going on.

By now you know I hate untested assumptions. However, here are some safe assumptions you can make, even if it turns out you're wrong:

- Assume everyone in the company has Google News Alerts turned on to "as it happens" for anything that pops on your company or executives.
- Assume employees are watching and/or participating in online forums for employees or the industry.
- Assume everyone is following your Facebook page, Twitter account, and LinkedIn page.

Communicate good news, neutral news, and bad news early and often—it's like voting in Chicago. Well-informed organizations tend to have less gossip, less time wasted on employees wondering "what if," and more trust of leadership and management, all of which help morale and productivity. Failing to communicate openly leads to employee frustration, conjecture, and inefficiency. Keep the lines of communication open by sharing the information you can, and by allowing questions in public and in private.

Don't Hide From What Can't Be Shared

Of course, not every piece of information can be shared willy-nilly. Personnel issues, contracts in negotiation, lawsuit details—this types of information is off limits for employee consumption. But don't hide from them. Explain that you can't discuss details yet, but will—if you can (personnel issues, for example, may never be appropriate to share)—at the earliest possible moment.

- If you don't know the answer to a question, don't make something up. Say you don't know, then explain how you'll find the answer and when you will share it.

- Every rational person knows that certain information can't be shared before its time. That time better be when or before people outside the company are told. Focus on keeping rational employees informed; exit irrational employees as soon as possible. For example, make sure you don't announce big strategic moves, big hires, promotions, or exits on social media platforms before you inform your staff. Address rumors as transparently as you can when they arise.
- Your first defense is a strong, informed employee base. Don't take it for granted that they live in the bubble of noninformation that would make your job so much easier. Pandora's box has been opened, and it will never close.

Transparency isn't just about gossip and news of the organization; transparency and clarity influence everything we do in the workplace. As I laid out in chapter 3, everyone's job should be clearly articulated and each person should know how his part of the work fits into the bigger picture.

At the far end of the transparency spectrum is open-book management, which has been advocated and described by John Case, author of *Open-Book Management* and *The Open-Book Experience*.[1] Case describes how some companies, such as Atlas Container Corp., operate their businesses with open books—employees have access to all the financials, and they have votes in certain critical decisions that impact them. Many companies run this way. It's a bold move that requires constant communication and education.

Whole Foods even lets employees look up any other employees' salaries, daily store sales data, and weekly regional sales data. CEO John Mackey believes that a "culture of shared information helps create a sense of 'shared fate' among employees." He eschews secrets because secrets don't create a "high-trust organization, an organization where people are all for one and one-for-all."[2]

I'm not quite ready for that level of open-book management at my company—it takes systems and capacity we need to build. However, we do share with the team lots of information other people might find excessive; we want everyone to understand how the business works and how each employee plays a part in our success.

Transparency takes constant communication, but it's worth it because it yields a team that gets what we do and why we're doing it. A variation on the Golden Rule works well: Tell your people—young and old—what you'd like to be told, as soon as you can.

Management Dos and Don'ts

- Do communicate the good news and the bad news to employees before they can hear it from people outside the organization.
- Do assume that everyone in your organization is reading Google Alerts about your company, its executives, and its competitors.
- Don't assume you can sweep bad news under the rug.
- Do answer questions honestly and openly. If you can't answer a question because it is legally sensitive, say so. When you can discuss it, do.

Millennial Dos and Don'ts

- Don't assume you're entitled to every scrap of information in the company.
- Don't assume everything you hear is true.
- Do ask open, positively framed questions.

11

A Full-Life Approach to Work

Work is a big part of my life; it needs to work FOR my life.

—*Mark, age twenty-nine*

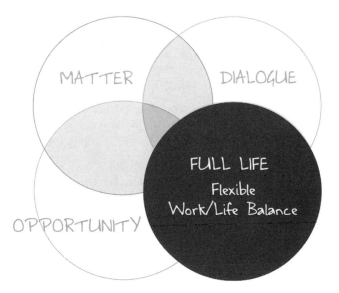

Flexible work programs. Job sharing. Working from home. Flex start times. These are all wonderfully intentioned policies that the workforce, young and old, increasingly wants. Many policies—written and implied—are in play across different industry sectors, in companies small and large throughout the country. But many have no such policies. And in some cases, as with Yahoo, flexible work options are being retracted because they've gotten out of hand and impacted performance and profitability, or at least the perception of performance and profitability.

Millennials are going to figure this work–life balance thing out eventually, as they grow into leadership positions. The companies that figure it out with and for them have, and will continue to have, a strategic advantage over those that don't.

As Gina, twenty-five, says so assertively, "I'm going to spend more time working than anything else as an adult. I don't want to wait until retiring to have a life—I want my work to be part of my life. And I definitely don't want to be like my parents, who both have jobs they really don't like and are waiting until they can retire to enjoy themselves."

The call for the elusive work–life balance has been a constant and increasingly loud drumbeat for the last twenty years, give or take a few years. Working women, with or without children, carried that drum for the first span of time, and in the last few years their working father counterparts have joined the chorus with increasing volume.

What impressed me during my research was the call for work–life balance now, at the beginning of their careers, by every single one of the Millennials I talked with—male, female, working, not yet working, parents, childless, married, single. They've joined the voices of working parents and working caretakers of aging parents who have been juggling life and work for a while now, and Millennials are pushing the boundaries on what it looks like to work and have a full life and not just work to live.

"I'm ambitious, but I'm willing to give some of that up if it means I can have a better life now," says Paul, twenty-seven, a high-performing CPA at a real estate private equity firm. While outliers exist on the perimeter, particularly in investment and management where big big money is in play, the general sentiment of Millennials seems to follow Paul's.

Younger   men   across   sectors—from   technology   to management consulting to finance—"increasingly want schedules that work around family needs—just as women have been demanding for years."[1] This sea change is even happening in medical schools.

This conviction stands in stark contrast to Harvard's recent survey[2] of C-level executives on the topic—that study showed that current top executives see work–life balance as an issue for women. That was true, even though 44 percent of the almost four thousand executives interviewed between 2008 and 2013 were women. The silver lining, as Jessie Grose writes on Slate, is that the Harvard Business School students who interviewed the executives "were dismayed by the findings. Both male and female students resisted the notion that you can't be an executive and also lead a balanced life."[3]

Technology and Remote Work

At the same time, advancing technology has made it possible to be connected yet distributed, and Millennials have grown up being educated with an increasingly sophisticated parade of technologies in the classroom. They are used to being connected by a virtual tether, not necessarily by their butts in the seats.

With robust cloud-based project management, work flow and storage systems available and priced for teams from one to one thousand, and effective one-to-one and group video conferencing systems and apps available at a wide range of price points, teams can have access to all of the information and processes they need to get the job done. "Why does my boss need to know where I am," asks Alice, twenty-eight. "I'm getting my work done—who cares if I'm not in the office?"

And here we step into the quicksand. "I personally struggle with how this approach can be so productive, when they're expecting so much at the outset," says Victoria, fifty-three. "We have to figure it out—but it's going to be messy."

Flexible Work Isn't The Same For Everyone

Not everyone can work from home or remotely whenever they like or all the time. If you're in a service business (and aren't we all, in some way) being available how and when the client or customer wants or needs you is required.

Some people work much more effectively and efficiently on certain tasks alone with no sounds to distract them, while others seem to disappear when they work remotely, and their work quality and efficiency on the same tasks suffers dramatically. For projects or work periods that demand a highly collaborative, high-performance approach and require fast, collective decisions and interdependent work, employees may need to be physically present, depending on the leader, the type of work, and the technology and systems available.

Bottom line, the companies that figure out how to offer some perceived freedom of movement and more flexible work policies will be the ones that attract and retain the future workforce. This is a strategic advantage now, and that advantage will grow as the number of Millennials becomes a larger and larger proportion of the workforce.

But it's not all that clear how to drive flexibility into the workplace in a way that works for everyone and is perceived as fair by everyone.

As my colleague Liz O'Donnell, author of the popular blog *HelloLadies.com* and the book *Mogul, Mom & Maid*, articulates so well, "If you want access to work–life benefits, you need to be able to negotiate for them and, more importantly, to prove that they work." And that's it. Flexible work schedules, access, benefits, and attitudes are a give and take.

By definition, flexible work schedules are inconsistent. It takes work to make them work—work on the employer's side and work on the employee's side. It takes intentional overcommunication to make sure everyone is on the same page.

But the benefits of flexible work arrangements can far outweigh the hassles. First, keeping great employees working with you as long as possible, through the ebbs and flows of their lives, maintains work continuity and performance. Second, employees are far more likely to be loyal to the team and company when the company flexes to accommodate their lives. The trick is to do it so that it doesn't impact team morale and overall performance.

The burden is on the employee to make it work—to make it work for him, his team, his clients, his customers, and the company. One bad apple can absolutely spoil it for everyone. A person who is hard to reach when working remotely, doesn't finish his work on time, doesn't tell his teammates his schedules during the workday, or has an attitude that assumes everyone else has to accommodate him puts the viability of the whole policy in jeopardy.

When Yahoo CEO Marissa Mayer changed the company's work-at-home policy, it came out that many people who had been on a work-from-home schedule couldn't be accounted for. The shift exposed a "great divide" in perception, as Forbes contributor Micheline Maynard[4] wrote, and uncovered resentment among people who worked from the office and knew that some who worked from home did not have their level of dedication.

My Own Story: A Company I Can Live With

We started my company in 2002, after my mother was diagnosed with stage-four lung cancer. At the time, I was in the running for two high-profile internal positions, and had no plans to start another agency. But when my mother was given three months to live, I withdrew from those searches and flew to Wisconsin to be with my parents as the family confronted this terrible news.

It became clear to me that, regardless of how my mother would take on and respond to her treatment, I required much more flexibility than any of the positions I was considering would allow. Eventually, my father would be a widower, living far from his three daughters who are spread out across the country. And my career could lend itself to owning my own company, where I could dictate the rules, thereby ensuring my ability to be there for my family. My longtime friend and colleague Dan and I cofounded our agency a couple of months after my mother's diagnosis.

My mother ended up living almost four more years, which was such a gift to us all. I spent more than thirty weeks of each of those years in Wisconsin, co-building my San Francisco-based company from more than two thousand miles away. I couldn't have done it if the people in San Francisco and I hadn't figured out together how to make it work. And if I took all the flexibility for myself, I would have found myself pretty much all alone—even in the down economy that the whole San Francisco Bay Area was in at that time. So our flexible attitude was born.

_____

Flexible Attitude

At the agency, we have a "flexible attitude." In practice, this means that people earn the privilege of working from home as many as three days per week (and sometimes more when circumstances require it) as long as the work allows. It also means they can handle personal e-mails during work hours and prioritize health and family—so they can attend kids' school functions and activities, make personal appointments to see a doctor, dentist, acupuncturist, or other provider during regular hours, and get to the gym or yoga studio regularly.

I value togetherness, and I actually prefer that everyone be in the office together all the time. But I am not able to do this, and if I want to have a single standard for all the employees I can hardly expect that everyone will want to do this. Our practice is that everyone come into the office on Tuesdays and

Thursdays, and that people schedule remote days as early as possible. We are all on IM during the day regardless of where we are physically, so that everyone can see who's "on" and who's "off." And if the team, the client, or the business requires people to be in the office, everyone's in the office. Period.

For the people who come into the office on Mondays, Wednesdays, and Fridays, we make sure there's a small perk that people at home will miss but not trade for being remote. For example, on Fridays we always have cocktails in the afternoon, and sporadically on Mondays or Wednesdays we'll bring in afternoon treats or lunches.

The UPS driver knows our office really well and can tell a lot about our shopping habits as people have their online purchases delivered to the office instead of their homes. This lets people be sure they get their packages, and they can return items from the office rather than having to schlep them back and forth and then work in going to the post office.

Compared to some larger companies, which offer on-site laundry services, on-site gyms, on-site day care, and free meals all day long, we come up short. However, those benefits are designed to keep people at the office as long as possible; our policy is designed to keep people at the office so they can work in close proximity regularly, but not all the time. We want to allow people to work remotely when we don't need them together to get the best work done.

This flexible attitude requires a strong team approach, constant communication, and robust reinforcement. And, most importantly, it requires trust and proof that we don't leave our teammates hanging just because we need or want a schedule that doesn't fit an uninterrupted nine-to-five workday.

Clif Bar & Company, a client, is famous for its culture and benefits. One flextime policy Clif Bar & Company has in place is the "9-80 work schedule," which allows employees to fit eighty hours of work into nine workdays. Effectively, this means that as much as half the company is off every Friday. It works for them—the company keeps growing.

Different divisions of large companies often have different policies, official or not, which match flexible schedules with the type of work done by different teams. "My team is spread out all over the world, so flexible schedules mean something different for us," explains Ted. "We need everyone to be together by video conference call a couple of times a month, which means someone's up late while others are up early. Other than that, each group in the team needs to come up with the work practices that work for them. We probably have four or five different 'policies' in place throughout the team, but it works."

In the end, it has to work. The work has to get done, on time, and to a high standard. Team members need to have confidence that everyone is being treated with an egalitarian hand, so that over time, everyone gets the same treatment and opportunity. And, yes, it's true that sometimes it takes getting back on the computer after the kids go to bed, or post yoga class, or after the water polo practice or the book group to make sure that all of the work is done, if you left at 4 p.m.

My Own Story: Juggling Life and Work

In my house, I am the CBO—Chief Bacon Officer—and my husband, Pete, who works half time, is the CHO—Chief Home Officer. I bring most of the money home, and my husband makes most things at home or in the family happen. Every working woman I know who knows my husband wants someone like him as her husband.

I feel compelled to say that I do contribute at home. I do tons of laundry, and put it away as well; I create and maintain the list of things that have to get done, which we collaborate on so that we (and by we, I mostly mean he) can get them done. I create the list of questions that need to be answered by our kids' teachers, instructors, doctors, and others. I manage all travel (which for us is quite a bit, with one child away at school and family spread out across the country), and more. But it's indisputable that my husband carries the load at home.... except for the laundry.

Pete shares his job with Abby, who also happens to be the mother of one of our younger son's classmates; Pete and Abby share car-pooling duties, getting our sons to their school about twenty miles away every day.

Ultimately, they don't just job share, they effectively co-parent our respective children. Our younger son and Abby's second son are both developmentally disabled, and require specific and consistent guidance throughout the day to have good days. During a thirty-minute drive each way to and from their special needs school, play dates, and as they help get our kids where they need to go after school, both Pete and Abby reinforce the behavior guidelines our kids need.

On paper this looks awesome. Two parents from different households share the same job, have two cars, and have two kids in the same grade at the same special needs school who are friends and who spend time after school together. Pete and Abby have perfected this arrangement, and Abby's husband and I look on with amazement over how they share so much, so well, to the benefit of their work and our sons.

Of course, as soon as either Abby's husband or I go out of town, it gets more challenging—and if we're both gone for business, then it's really hairy, because invariably someone gets sick and the schedule goes to hell. But each family leans on the other to make it all work, and Pete and Abby lean on each other to make their one job work. It takes a village, and both families feel so fortunate that we have this luxury.

Paving the Way

In some cases, older employees who have been pushing hard for flexible options for a long time and have finally earned the right to a flexible work schedule are bitter that their younger colleagues are getting now what they worked so hard for over their careers. "It's taken me fifteen years to get to be able to regularly work from home—I've had to overdeliver to prove the point that I can do the job and not always be there, and these kids want this flexibility now," complains Abby. "And I don't see any of them overdelivering like I had to."

Those who have paved the way for flexible work schedules and now begrudge the people who follow them need to get over it. Thank you for all your hard work. Thank you for proving the point that working remotely can be done well. You've made it possible for companies to make these changes. Your kids have watched you and want what you worked so hard for now—you've taught them what is possible, and they know it can work. Just because we didn't have more flexible work plans when we started our careers doesn't mean we shouldn't allow the younger generation what we know is a good thing for them and for the business.

At the same time, everyone, regardless of age or situation, needs to make sure she doesn't take flexibility for granted. Clear policies and guidelines about how to make flexibility and freedom work will help anyone, of any age, from feeling or projecting an attitude of entitlement.

"She just told me that she'd be out all afternoon for a doctor's appointment," says Michael, thirty-six, a product manager in a California-based produce company, talking about a recent declaration from one of his twenty-four-year-old direct reports. "And this was one that she'd scheduled weeks before. She didn't think to ask if it was okay that she'd be gone. She hadn't bothered to check the deadline schedule to make sure her being out wasn't going to trip up the whole team. It turned out that it was okay, but I was really put out that she just assumed that she could go."

When, during our call, Michael asked for advice on how to "correct this behavior," I asked a few questions.

> **Lee:** "Is there a policy that you have to ask before you take time during the day?"
> **Michael:** "Well, it's just common courtesy."
> **Lee:** "Does everyone else ask before they take time out of work during the day?"
> **Michael:** "I'm not sure."
> **Lee:** "Have you ever told her what you expect from her when she needs or wants to shift her work schedule around?"
> **Michael:** [Silence.]

What's common courtesy to one person is implied or assumed by others, and not necessarily because they're feeling entitled. I think most often it's because they simply do not know what is expected.

Sue, another senior leader, fifty-one, shared her story about her twenty-nine-year old direct report's regular texts to her.

> **Nancy:** "Hi. Bus is late again. I will be in by ten. Will call into the conference call from bus and mute to listen."
> **Sue:** "Okay."

This text interchange and variations thereof went on for weeks. Sue assumed "that she'd figure it out that this was not okay," but nothing changed until Sue texted back one day: "When are you going to figure out you need to get an earlier bus?" Nancy replied, "Oh yeah." And Nancy hasn't been late for meetings since.

Guidelines Are Imperative

Again, what's obvious to some remains elusive to others, even when they don't make their commitments. Without guidelines and reinforcement about what's important and about the procedure required to get flexibility, you may be disappointed and angry about how other people interpret a flexible policy.

Companies and their leaders must put guidelines behind flexible work policies that help everyone comply without leaving teammates hanging out to dry or having to pick up someone else's work to get the team's job done. This becomes very important when we need to deal with our employees' life emergencies. When teams have a history of being able to flex during regular life activities, they are much more capable of navigating during times of personal emergency. If each person is confident that, when he has something urgent occur in his life, the team will cover him too, team members move much more easily to fill a gap created by an emergency.

Finally, an egalitarian approach to flexible work schedules does not necessarily mean that everything is *equal*. Different people work best in different conditions, and different roles have different requirements. Some positions require that the employees filling them always be present; others do not. If someone demonstrates that she can't work remotely and be effective, then bring her back, and help her earn the right to try again. We need to adjust given both the work at hand and the people at hand.

It would certainly be easier if everyone would just show up regularly, on time, and not even ask for any accommodation. But that train has left the station and is not returning. We need to work together to make it work.

So What Do You Do?

I've reviewed more than two dozen flexible work policies and the only thing they have in common is that they each allow work outside 9 a.m. – 5 p.m. in the office standard. Each organization needs to find the flexible work policies and guidelines that work for its own work style, conditions and business mandates. Write them down, and know that you may need to adjust the guidelines more than once to get it right so that they work. Follow these guidelines to get you started:

1. Identify what "flexible work plan" means to your employees:
   - Shorter workweeks? (e.g., 4-40, 9-80, etc.)
   - Work from home anywhere from one to five days per week?
   - Flexible hours (e.g., come in early, leave early; leave early, log in late from home, etc.)
2. Identify what works for your business:
   - When do your customers expect you/your employees to be available? Do they need to see you in person? Can you check in by phone? Online?
   - Who works better in the office? Who works better doing certain work at home? Do different teams need different conditions given the different types of work and information they need?
3. Identify any positions that cannot be done remotely. In what ways can you build some "flex" into these positions? (e.g., a two-hour lunchtime to accommodate errands or gym time, a later start and end time, an earlier start and end time? etc.)
4. Choose the technologies or systems you need to make flexible work work:
   - Project management service?
   - A customer relationship management (CRM) system?
   - Closed social networks (e.g., Yammer, Jive)
5. Decide on rules of engagement that need to be articulated so that flexible work schedules create more efficiency and productivity, not questions about what people are doing. For example:
   - Update team members on your flex schedule daily
   - Use IM status bar to indicate availability
   - Set deadlines for the team in the office, not the person working late that day

6. Have a plan for addressing policies that are not working. This means you must articulate how you will specifically know when the flex policy is not working. For instance:
   - Deadlines are met late at night requiring attention by people who have already finished their work days
   - Key people are not available when their teams need them or at decision times
   - Everyone is waiting on the person who is off-schedule and can't move forward without their approval or participation

Address these issues immediately; do not let them fester or discontent will take root and grow. Use the circle of communication to help come to new agreements and arrangements.

7. If you have to, revoke flexible work schedules until the employee has proven he can work efficiently and well within the regular work hours. Then give them back one step at a time as he proves he can work well with the team off schedule or off site.

Remember, one size does not fit all people or all workplaces!

Management Dos and Don'ts

- Do articulate and put in writing your expectations for people's presence in the office. Be specific about start and stop times. Be specific about when people need to be present.
- Do set a policy and provide specific guidelines about how to deviate from the regular schedule.
- Don't assume that everyone will just "get it" and know when they need to be there or how to get permission or inform their managers about time away from the office.
- Do lead by example: show people how to flex their time effectively by overcommunicating your schedule and how

you will get your work done in time without requiring other people to change their schedules.

- Do put in systems that facilitate remote and shared work. Consider using Basecamp, SharePoint, Box, or other cloud- or server-based systems to share work information securely from anywhere.
- Do *ask* what people want. Do give people the reasons you have your policy.
- Do be reasonable. Let people prove that they can make it work.
- Do be consistent.

Millennial and anyone else with a flexible schedule Dos and Don'ts

- Don't assume the work policy is without reason.
- Do negotiate for flextime rationally by articulating how you will make it work, not drop the ball, and get your work done.
- Don't assume you can just take the time off.
- Do ask, "Is it okay if I take off early today? I'll make it up tonight."
- Don't assume, just because there isn't a written policy, that rules don't exist.
- Do get your work done on time and well. Better yet, be early! Prove that you can work remotely without letting the work slide.
- Do let people know how to reach you if you are working remotely.
- Don't make people chase you when they can't see you.
- Do understand that "egalitarian" does not necessarily mean "equal." Different people work best in different conditions. Some positions require that employees be present; others do not.
- Do think before you complain.

12

Access Up the Chain

I'm going to go to the person who can help me most.
—*Stephanie, age twenty-six*

Hierarchy is an anachronistic concept for many Millennials. Having grown up one click away from seemingly all the information in the world, the ability to mobilize a dispersed group with social media, and the ability to democratize media with their own channels and information curation, Millennials see the work world as a much flatter place than Baby Boomers or Gen Xers did when they were in their twenties and thirties.

"Millennials don't see structure at all. When they do, they see structure as a ceiling not a floor—they see structure that gets in the way of their hopes and dreams," says Chris, fifty-four.

When asked to rank how important access to senior management is in the job, nine out of ten of the hundred-plus twenty-two- to thirty-four-year-olds I talked with or surveyed placed regular access to leadership at the top of the list. Ted, a senior leader in a large multinational software company, laughs, "Access to people above me? Oh yeah! My guys go around me and talk to anyone they want to all the time. But they take it to an extreme. They just go and do it without any preparation or thought process."

On the one hand, explains Ted, "It's good that they feel the freedom to talk with anyone in the organization. On the other hand, they don't understand that they could have such a better reaction if they were sponsored or helped."

Marty, CEO of a midsized company in Seattle, says, "Sometimes I feel ambushed. I want to have an open-door policy and be supportive of everyone, but there's no way I can answer their questions about their prospects or opportunities well all the time. I wish they'd tee up their conversation with their managers so I could be helpful and constructive instead of just shooting in the dark."

Ted adds, "I get a lot of 'What the hell was that?' from the people above me, and have to do a lot of interpretation of what my bosses meant when they are approached by the people below me. I really need to hit them over the head with a two by four sometimes so they don't hear encouragement as a promise of advancement."

Of course, there are lots of benefits of providing access. First, it helps senior leaders keep a pulse on what is going on with the front line of the company—how the work flow is changing with junior employees' input and what is on their minds. Second, when done authentically, it helps break down barriers between people at different levels and ease communication channels, to help keep everyone pointed in the right direction.

I subscribe to Daniel Goleman's notion that "the fundamental task of leaders is to prime good feeling in those they lead."[1] Providing direct access from employees to people in leadership positions is the first order of business in achieving this. At the same time, it's not very constructive or efficient for leadership at any level in the organization to spend all of their time giving audiences to everyone around them. And nothing undermines other leaders and managers in the organization more than not reinforcing some sort of structure and reporting authority.

Each organization—in fact, each leader—needs to find a balance with regard to access in their culture. What will it look like? What is the standard? What is special? What is the goal of access?

I can answer that last question for you. The goal of providing access is to reinforce the culture of the organization, to provide a forum to hear ideas from those people closest to the work, and to provide informal mentorship to younger, less experienced colleagues.

Even though my small, thirty-five-person organization has an open floor plan and I sit in the crowd, I do not hear or notice everything. I think some of my team must wonder why things are news to me when I'm first looped in on a topic. When you get to a size when you can't see everyone, that complicates things further. If you add in multiple offices in different time zones, you exponentialize the potential for miscommunication.

Over the last twenty years, I've worked with more than a hundred C-level leadership executives and teams in companies of different sizes and cultures, and it's easy to see the difference between those that feel empowered by the free flow of ideas and constructive feedback among different levels in the organization, and those that do not.

Energy is the key differentiator. The energy in the room, the energy of the people, the energy of a project that moves forward easily even if it's hard, because the people are well connected to the mission and vision and leaders of the organization. And access to leadership—perceived, even if not acted upon—plays a large role, particularly with Millennials, who see it as an essential part of a satisfying job.

Access Requires Feedback

However, access without a closed feedback loop is worse than useless, it's demotivating and destructive. "He has an open-door policy, but everyone knows it's a black hole where good ideas go to die," says Michael, thirty-three, of how his CEO puts—or fails to put—the access idea into practice. Not that you have to solve everyone's problems or give immediate answers or implement every idea. The unwritten contract of productive access is to provide a way to gather and then address the information you receive. It would be better to refuse access to people if you don't plan to loop back with a "thank you," answers, next steps, or a rationale for why someone's ideas aren't going to be implemented.

Unless it's an urgent personnel, customer service, or legal issue, do not promise immediate consideration. One senior leader I talked with gathers all of the non-urgent feedback over the course of a month, presents it to his direct reports, and then, with them, gives feedback with the broader team in a meeting held at the end of the month. This way, he bubbles up themes and shows how some things resolved on their own, others evolved into ideas that were implemented, and still others require more thought or time.

If you're in the leadership seat, make sure you give closure or next steps to the different topics that arise during these access times, and be sure to loop in other people in the reporting chain. (If you're the person who has availed herself of senior leadership's time, make sure you say thank you and follow up with any action items discussed.)

Access That Works

An open-door policy alone won't help you achieve your goals or provide constructive access to Millennials and other workers who want your time. So how can you build a culture of constructive access? Find several avenues to sharing information and getting input. Provide ways to give advice and guidance on urgent and not-so-urgent matters that support your direct reports. Share your vision widely.

Practically speaking, what does this look like? Some of it depends on the size of the organization. Effective leadership needs to happen everywhere in the organization, through and with different people. Effective leadership is not silent and it is not infrequent.

Consider a different matrix of ways to be a present and accessible leader who keeps people informed, provides access, and walks that line between overly processed and agile and empowered.

All-Hands Meetings

Monthly all-hands meetings at which senior leaders provide updates on the business, have some fun, and shine a light on progress keep people in touch with management, their personalities, and their vision.

One client held a monthly all-hands at HQ the first Friday of every month to review progress, highlight successes, address issues and answer any question from the floor—and there were some doozy questions over the years. His willingness to answer every question in public was highly prized by the staff of more than 350 people at headquarters. He ended each meeting with a reminder of the vision—why everyone was there and a charge or goal for the coming month. Everyone knew where he stood and what mattered most.

Weekly E-mails

If you don't see your whole team weekly, consider adding a Friday afternoon check-in to update your team on the previous week or two—what's moved forward, any staff news, and wins or initiatives underway. If you're part of a management team, consider sharing this duty among yourselves.

Dr. Jeff Boehm, executive director of the Marine Mammal Center, a leading care and research facility for marine mammals and ocean health in Sausalito, California, sends a weekly e-mail on Fridays to the center's more than 1,500 employees, volunteers, board members, and key partners. He updates everyone on what has happened that week—rescues, how many animals the hospital is caring for, trends in the patients and implications, milestones met, etc. He keeps his wide-ranging (the center covers six hundred miles of California coastline) army of volunteers and staff abreast of events and feeling connected. Each week, he gets a handful of responses, and everyone knows that they can respond to him and that he will return their e-mails as soon as he is able.

Open-Door Policy

My assistant's number-one charge is to get anyone in my organization who wants my time onto my calendar as fast as possible, and move other people around if he needs to, to make my employee meetings happen; next on the priority list are my clients who want my time; and then come the people connected to the organizations of which I am a member of the board. Then everyone else. Employees first. (Actually, his number-one charge is to make sure my family gets what they need from me during the day, but that's a small group and they don't call often—employees are a close second.)

Group Lunches

Consider taking small groups of people (five to seven) from throughout the organization to lunch—or at least sitting with them over pizza in the office—once a month. Get to know those people's interests. Probe them on satisfaction. Ask direct questions such as, "Is there anything you think we could be doing better?" "Is there something we're doing well we should do more of?" "Is there something you'd like to see me do differently?"

Staff Education and Training

Share your knowledge, your expertise, and your special sauce with your team through training sessions on those topics that support the culture (how to give feedback), your company's mission, and/or skills (presentation, writing, and so on). Make a video of the session and create a learning channel on your company intranet so you can share your own special sauce with new people. Have everyone participate over time to broaden the library and share different expertise for the benefit of all.

Closed Social Circles

Create a closed Facebook group or Google Circle, or use another closed social platform such as Jive or Yammer. Post regularly:

- Questions; moderate the resulting dialogue
- Updates
- Pictures from your day

Anniversary Lunch

If you're the CEO of one of the 5.8 million[2] companies in the United States with fewer than fifty people, consider taking each team member to an informal lunch on her work anniversary. Make sure everyone understands this is not a performance review, but rather a personal thank you from the boss. Ask open-ended questions about the person's job, her feelings about the company, whether she has any ideas about how the company could improve, or what good things the company should do more of, in her opinion. Make sure you keep track of ideas and sentiments that come up during lunch. Look for trends that need to be addressed widely and ideas that will improve performance, the fun quotient, and collaboration.

If you manage teams larger than thirty, consider sharing the anniversary lunch with other senior leaders in the group.

Walk 'n' Talk

Author and business advisor Nilofer Merchant captured an important concept in 2013, when she presented at TED on walking meetings. "Sitting is the smoking of our generation," says Nilofer. I was so inspired by Nilofer's talk that we started encouraging "Walk 'n' Talk" meetings last year. Even one thirty-minute Walk 'n' Talk per week can yield more than seventy-five extra miles walked in a year, and who wouldn't benefit from that?! Put one or two thirty-minute Walk 'n' Talks on your calendar every week and let anyone in the company schedule them with you. By walking side by side instead of sitting across from each other at a desk or table, you've removed the temptation to watch your phone and, for some people, taken away the stress of having to look the boss in the eye while sharing their thoughts.

Surprise and Delight

"Surprise and delight" campaigns are all the rage with consumer products companies, but the place to put at least some of your surprise and delight energies is with your employees. Every once in a while, surprise and delight your team. And take a little time to be with them during the delight part.

- Do a Slurpee run in the afternoon.
- Bring in breakfast for the whole team.
- Make ice cream cookie sandwiches and pass them out.
- Find a toy or game you particularly like, and buy one for each of your teammates; I personally love the Magic 8

Ball and the "Yes" and "No" buttons that yell out different ways to affirm or deny.

- Schedule a meeting and take them bowling instead.
- Occasionally, take teammates out for drinks.

In the end, people want your time and your ideas, and it's up to you to make it productive for the organization, the person sitting in front of you, and yourself. The more you can provide multiple avenues for constructive access, the more your young teammates will be engaged with your company and the more you will be able keep your finger on the pulse of the organization. Giving effective access is admirable and desired work with a positive payoff.

Management Dos and Don'ts

- Do find ways to be accessible for people of all ages and responsibility levels on your team.
- Do share what you know with people coming up through the organization. Give the gift of your knowledge to others who could benefit from it.
- Do leverage any time you spend in training or presenting by taking video and putting it up for future use.
- Don't give all of your time away. Carve some time every week or month to be available to the staff and let people see you then unless an urgent issue demands your attention earlier.
- Do consider adding Walk 'n' Talks to your schedule every week.

Millennial Dos and Don'ts

- Don't assume going over your boss's head will be welcomed.
- Do engage your manager in what you want to get out of meeting with his boss. Ask him to help you get the most out of this time.

- Do be prepared, if you ask for time, to present your ideas clearly and concisely and provide backup.
- Don't be upset if the person you want to see can't see you right away. People are busy for a reason, and that reason most likely has nothing to do with you.

13

Mutual Mentorship

> There's a special place in hell for women and men who don't help each other.
>
> —Michelle, age twenty-five (quoting
> Secretary of State Madeleine Albright)

A 2012 Dimensional Research survey revealed that mentorship was the number one request by Millennials worldwide, with 42 percent requesting help finding a mentor.[1] In my discussions with more than one hundred Millennials across the United States, mentorship came up eight out of ten times, right behind access to senior management. "Young people want to be mentored," says Jennifer, twenty-seven. "All of my friends have mentors and we share what our mentors share with us with each other."

Mentorship is obviously not a new phenomenon, but what today's young mentees want out of their mentor relationship has shifted a bit. Mentees still want mentors to open doors and give guidance and advice, as Caitlin the twenty eight year old from Seattle notes, but they don't necessarily want to follow in their mentor's shoes. "I asked one of my mentors how I could avoid having to work like he does. He was a bit surprised with the question. But I don't want to be him. I want to understand what he has had to do so I can figure out what path I should take that is not his," shared Caitlin.

Carol, fifty-four, echoes the sentiment from the other side of the desk. "I mentor a couple of younger people at work but neither wants to have my job. They want me to help them—they are eager and willing to listen—but they don't want to work the way my job and life demands."

My Own Experience:
Shift from Mother to Daughter

In the mid-1970s my mother, a Phi Beta Kappa graduate of Brown University (then Pembroke), sat at our kitchen table for months, learning how to type so she could go to business school. It took months, because the self-help book could only be paid attention to in between managing the house, caring for her three very different daughters with very different interests, taking on leadership roles at our school's PTA and our church, walking the dogs (because the kids were too busy), oh, and doing that wife thing.

She graduated from the first Simmons (all women) MBA program at age forty-one as Salutatorian and embarked on a successful banking career. Once she had her first job, she consistently drilled into my head that finding male mentors who would help "break down the walls" for women was key to women having "meaningful careers in business, like men."

The prevailing notion was that male mentors would help my mother and other working women rise to get the same jobs—and the same conditions—that men had. That was in 1976, and clearly we still have a long way to go on that gender equality thing.

On one hand, mentors are not to be confused with parents—particularly parents who are overly involved in their children's careers. On the other hand, some young mentees have a hard time distinguishing between the kind of support a parent could give (or really should not give) and the type of support an older mentor can and should give. It's up to the mentor to course correct the relationship if it strays into parenting.

Mentors need to be supportive, and it's important to set expectations and boundaries so that they can provide a constructive, professionally helpful relationship without allowing the dynamic to slip into that of a parental relationship. "I've seen a shift in how some of the younger workers approach me as a mentor in the last few years," says Anne, forty-eight, who has regularly mentored younger colleagues over the last fifteen years. "I've had to redirect some of my more recent mentees to approach me in my role as their mentor with more structure and less like a parent."

We can't underestimate the mutual benefits of a constructive mentor-mentee relationship for both parties. For mentors, the satisfaction of helping someone else achieve her goals is undeniable. And what's not good about the karma mentors are putting into the universe by paying it forward or paying back the time their mentors invested in them?

Millennial Insight: Jennifer, age twenty-five

"I think it's cool when experienced people reach out and offer to be a mentor," says Jennifer. Older generations, according to Jennifer, "have a lot to teach and we have a ton to learn from you. Passing on your legacy, being able to coach someone is pretty awesome."

At the same time, mentoring younger colleagues provides a window into the mind-set, challenges, pressures, and lifestyle of the younger workforce, allowing us to better understand them. And, importantly, mentoring provides an instant tap into a mentee's network of friends and peers, which we might need to find future junior employees, particularly for smaller organizations that do not have a robust recruiting function in-house.

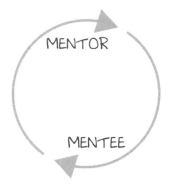

Most of us will need younger connections in the next ten to fifteen years to keep us relevant. And who knows, we might be counting on them for a referral, or even hiring us, in the future. With so much emphasis being placed on the quality of the team and the access to senior people by job-searching Millennials, having a leg up with a peer endorsement goes a long way in recruiting efficiently and well.

How to Be a Good Mentor

Mentors help fill knowledge gaps and find ways to help their mentees grow. There are a number of things to keep in mind as you embark on a mentor relationship with a younger person. As Pamela Ryckman, author of *Stiletto Network* explains, a great mentor "is honest and unafraid to tell you hard truths about yourself and your work . . . , [and she] pushes you to take risks and aim higher." Importantly, a great mentor at the same workplace "advocates for you when you're not there."[2]

Purpose

Many mentor relationships fail because they lack purpose or definition. Is this a more prescriptive relationship, with the senior person imparting knowledge focused on career development in a mostly one-way learning experience? Or is it a more developmental relationship focused on "growing the less experienced person's capability" by requiring the mentee to do things for him- or herself?[3] Define the role you are willing to take on with your mentee and what you expect during the engagement.

Time and Place

Agreeing to be a mentor is a responsibility and a time commitment. What kind of time can you commit to a mentee? Remember, mentorship need not happen in person; phone, e-mail, or Skype all can work well to keep you connected during a mentorship period in place of, or in between, in-person meetings.

Time Frame and Frequency

Consider a defined time frame, one you are confident you can fulfill, for the initial mentorship relationship, instead of an unconditionally implied "forever."

Meetings once a month for a year? If you cannot commit to a long engagement, consider a short, prescribed mentorship on a narrow topic. Can you manage three meetings over two months with e-mails a few times in between?

Rules of Engagement

1. Mentorships are confidential relationships. "A mentor is someone with whom you can let down your guard, share your insecurities, and ask the 'stupid' questions we all have sometimes," says Pamela Ryckman.[4]
2. Be willing to share your experience and knowledge.
3. Give thoughtful, candid, and constructive feedback. Be direct. Be encouraging.
4. Do not do your mentee's job for him. An active ear, direction, and constructive feedback should not cross the line into managing or chasing down the mentee, or doing the heavy lifting he needs to do to achieve his goals.
5. End every session on an upbeat note.

Listen and Ask Questions

Useful mentorships are not platforms for pontification. Instead, they are coaching relationships that help the mentee define her own way through her career. Listen with an active and non-judgmental ear.

Consider keeping the discussion as elevated as possible by asking the same questions during each session, such as:

1. What's your biggest challenge right now? (Probe on priorities and reasons.)
2. What are you doing to address it? (Probe on problem solving.)
3. What learning do you need to address it? What are you reading? What should you be reading?

Resist the urge to solve any problems that come up quickly. Instead, help your mentee peel the onion on the issue at hand, and come to her own conclusion about a way forward. At the same time, don't let her flounder along, grasping at straws. Point her in the right direction and set the expectation for better preparation next session.

Narrow Mentorships

If you have only a small window of time, narrow the topic of the mentorship to a single issue and plan on frequent sessions in that small window to allow for iteration and "homework" in between meetings. Sample topics that work well in narrow, short-term mentorships include client management, strategic counseling, business strategy, career planning, and so on.

Mentees of all ages: if you're looking for a mentor these seven steps will help you identify and engage a person who can help make a difference for you.

1. Define what you want out of a mentorship. General career advancement advice? Specific knowledge? A sounding board?

2. Identify the right person—someone who has experience, position, and the respect of others, and who is not so removed from your position that she can't relate. Choose someone just barely out of your league.[5] This person could be inside or outside your company. If you can't find the "right" person among the people you already know, leverage your LinkedIn network to find and get connected to one or several "right" people.

3. Approach the person you hope will take you on with a specific request; be prepared to explain why you chose the person, what you hope to get out of a mentorship, and what kind of time commitment you are hoping for. Be ready to detail how you will prepare for any meetings and ask for any restrictions or preferences the person may have. If your preferred mentor cannot commit to you, ask for a recommendation of someone she thinks would be a good fit.

4. Respect your mentor's time. It's your responsibility to manage the relationship—to set up and confirm meetings; to be prepared; to prepare your mentor in the way he requests so he can more easily help you; and to fulfill any agreements you make.

5. Be intentional and proactive. This isn't a lunch to chitchat or talk sports. This is a meeting with a professional purpose.

6. Protect your mentor. Don't abuse the relationship by freely connecting your friends and network to your mentor.

7. Remember, your mentor is not your parent.

Mutual Mentorship

Boomers and Gen Xers can also ask Millennials to be their mentors on specific topics. If you continue to be flummoxed by Instagram or Pinterest, or don't know how to use Facebook or blog comments to your advantage, consider having a

Millennial colleague or acquaintance mentor you for a month or two.

Ask your mentee what she reads regularly, and read those blogs and newsfeeds to get a good sense of the information and sources that are informing your younger colleagues' points of view. Copy their Pulse or FlipBook feeds and page through daily for a month or two—your frame of reference will expand and you will have better insight into how Millennials think.

You will learn a lot and, assuming you do it well, you will be setting a great example of how Millennials should conduct their own mentoring relationships.[6]

Management Dos and Don'ts

- Do accept at least one Millennial's request for mentorship for at least a short time.
- Don't become a "second parent" to a Millennial mentee.
- Do establish clear boundaries and rules of engagement for the mentor/mentee relationship.
- Don't do your mentee's work for him.
- Do ask your Millennial mentee for help in something you don't do well.
- Do read what your mentee reads.

Millennial Dos and Don'ts

- Do be thoughtful about who you ask to be your mentor. Why him? To learn what? For how long?
- Do drive the relationship.
- Don't make the mentor have to chase you down.
- Do prepare for each meeting or session. Be specific in your ask.
- Don't share your mentor's contact information with your network.
- Do read what your mentor reads.
- Do say thank you.

14

Outline Career Path Options

If good people don't see how they can progress through their career with you, they won't join you or stay with you.

—*Jenna, age forty-four, human resources director*

I subscribe to the "Captain, My Captain"[1] philosophy of career management, that leaders can inspire and show, and that individuals need to take responsibility for their own decisions, values, and actions; everyone should watch *The Dead Poet's Society*[2] once or twice as an adult to keep inspired. I believe that people have the ultimate responsibility in driving their own career where they want it to go. I say this as a mother of two sons: one an optimistic, talented musician on his own not-so-easy (and oh-so-unexpected by his parents) path to touch many people through his work and gift, and the other an energetic, developmentally disabled force for good in the world who will most likely never be independent.

The best companies provide opportunity for learning and advancement, but that advancement is earned not given. I think people should stay at companies as long as they are contributing positively and are either happy with what they're doing or are contributing to the company's work while learning something that may take them elsewhere.

If someone wants to bide her time in a job, that's fine as long as she is contributing. If someone wants to step back from the growth path and limit his hours so he can be very active in his children's lives, take care of an aging parent, or have more free time to pursue different activities, that's fine too, as long as he can make it work for the company.

The most important thing for me is that people who work at my company have pride in their time with us and can point to their employment with us as an advantage in their career. And while I don't expect anyone to stay with us forever, I do hope that those who have worked at the firm will be positively connected to us once they've left.

Millennial Insight: Liz, age twenty-nine

"In my experience, Gen Xers and Millennials more often than not share the belief that they are responsible for their own happiness."

We help those people who tell us that they feel their career path is not accommodated by our business: either we find a way to accommodate that path in our business because it is good for the business, or we help them by connecting them with people we know or by doing something else helpful.

I believe that the good people always come back, either as employees, as clients, or as referrals. Actually, I know this: many people currently working at my firm are repeaters, having worked with me or someone else on the staff earlier in their careers, or they are former clients. Most new clients are referred by current or former clients, several of whom are former employees.

When employees ask me, "What is my career path here?" I always answer with "What do you want it to be?" When potential employees ask me, "What are my career options here?" I always answer with "What do you want to do? Let's see if that fits with what we do or plan to do." I'm sure this is irritating to some, and I've gotten many a blank stare from candidates in the twenty-two to twenty-seven-year-old range, but it helps frame the way forward, not as my or the company's responsibility, but as theirs.

Gen X Insight: Ted, age forty-seven

"I recently had a one-on-one meeting with a woman in her late twenties or early thirties who said to me, 'You know and I know that I'm not going to be here forever, so what's the next best thing I can do here? Help me figure this out so I can have a great experience before I'm done.' I was dumbstruck for a moment and told her I'd have to think on it. At first I was pissed, but then I figured out that she just said out loud what everyone is probably thinking. After a week we met again and I mapped out how she could be valuable to the team and get value for herself out of some expanded roles over the next twelve to eighteen months. I also made it clear that I expect 100 percent participation during this time. She was happy; I've gotten the promise for some good work. I hope it works out."

Why Should I Work Here?

In the past few years, even during a really tough job environment, the question "Why should I work here?" has been asked in interviews by recent college graduates, even though almost no candidate gets to me without significant vetting.

When I first started hearing this a few years ago I'm sure my face did not disguise my astonishment or insult at the question. Now I know that many Millennials are being counseled to ask this and other, similar questions. So instead of dropping my jaw in disbelief, I now say, "You shouldn't if you don't want to...[long pause]...and aren't ready for the work."

Usually, people either laugh out loud or sit in silence. And then I continue: "But if this the career you think you want to pursue and you have initiative, if you are a good team player and are curious, if you have a sense of humor and can write a compelling, logical paragraph or two, I can't think of a better place to work for people…[long pause]…who qualify."

Career Development

In terms of promotions, I operate with the point of view that promoting people before they are ready for that next level is a disservice to the employee and the team—it sets everyone up for failure. Managers need to work with employees to articulate a specific plan for improvement and for skill and experience building in as aggressive a time frame as makes sense for that person. If the employee doesn't make it, he doesn't make it, but at least you have worked with him to help him achieve his goals.

While Millennials often talk about wanting a career path and development opportunities, many companies have found a maddening disconnect between that stated desire and the initiative different individuals take, or don't take, around their own education and development. "We offer so many training opportunities, all tied to moving up the ladder, and we can't get any of our under-thirty crowd to take advantage of them," says Matt, fifty-two, an executive vice president at a large marketing firm, echoing the sentiments of many of the senior leaders I talked with. "It's like pulling teeth to get them to go and pay attention," he says. Not to mention getting them to actually apply what they've supposedly learned in the training sessions.

"I just paid for one of my up-and-comers to go to an advanced writing class, and the first assignment she got afterward showed no difference," bemoans Margaret. "And this after she got high marks from the instructor. It makes no sense to me."

In discussions that resembled tales of walking uphill both ways to and from school in subzero weather through the driving snow, manager after manager talked about how many of their younger colleagues don't do the "things we just knew to do when we were coming up the ladder."

Part of me thinks this is a bit of historical fiction. The other part of me concurs. I shared this frustration until I stopped hitting my head against the wall and decided to provide incentives for people to learn—for their own professional advancement and for the sake of the company's continuing relevance and value.

One night I was cashing in my American Express rewards points for shopping gift cards and it hit me that the answer was in front of me. I'd award points to people who took classes and applied the learning to their work, sharing and putting what they learned into action. Thus, the Double Forte Rewards Program was born. Now our people earn points for attending webinars, brown-bag presentations, training sessions, and internal and external workshops. We also give employees points for related college-level classes and will pay for the class if they score an 85 percent or higher. We give more points to people who share their wisdom with others in online tutorials or in one-to-one or group training sessions.

While we've provided a range of "cash in" options, most people choose to hoard points until they reach a value between $250 and $500 so that they can go to a special restaurant, get great seats at a concert or performance, or purchase an iPad or other tablet for home. Going at a good clip, earning that many points takes anywhere between three and five months.

In the two years since we introduced the rewards program, the number of training and career development classes and courses that people give and take has exploded by more than 350 percent, and everyone, including our clients, has benefitted from the work. To pay for the program, I've factored the rewards into the overall benefits line on the P&L. Those people who do more, get more. Everyone has the same opportunity.

Millennial Insight: Adam, age thirty

"To my fellow Millennials: you don't have to have the word 'manager' in your job titles to have a chance to demonstrate your leadership skills.

"You have to take the initiative and sell out leadership opportunities in every job you have. As you progress in your career, take leadership classes and attend seminars. Read reputable books or articles on the topic. Do all this while you are still in the early years of your career so when you do become a manager and lead others, you won't be blindsided by the challenges that come with it. You need to build up your leadership experience to have leadership skills."[3]

Job-Hoppers

While Millennials are often considered "job-hoppers" by their older colleagues, the last decade has been fraught with uncertain conditions that have strengthened the belief that people are in charge of their own careers and should not count on companies keeping their positions on the payroll. "Workers today know they could be laid off any time—after all, they saw it happen with their parents—so they plan defensively and essentially consider themselves 'free agents,'" explains Jeanne Meister, a workplace consultant.[4]

"Every person under thirty I have in my network has an ear cracked to new opportunities," says Leslie, the GenX recruiter. You can't stop someone else's open ear or seemingly constant searching. What you can do is focus on making your team and your company as good as it can be—from the people to the culture to the work and the performance. If we operate in fear of people leaving us, we're playing from a disadvantage. By playing small, we may make the mistake of bending the rules for individuals in a way that does not make sense for the business and creates disharmony among the staff.

If we operate to maximize our team's engagement, we hold onto people longer, and they become assets to the company over the long term. If people aren't contributing, they need to go. If you find ways for more people to contribute with their different goals, experiences, and preferences, you win.

Management Dos and Don'ts

- Do focus on creating a culture of earned opportunity.
- Don't overreact when candidates approach their interviews with what you might consider an entitled attitude.
- Do set expectations early for how people advance in your team and company.
- Do find ways for your growth-seeking employees to learn new things.
- Do insist on employees mastering skills and proficiency before they take on new tasks or responsibilities.

Millennial Dos and Don'ts

- See chapter 6 on interviewing questions.
- Do know that no one owes you a career.
- Do perform your job well and master the tasks at hand.
- Do use your time in a position well, fully contributing in your role.
- Do share your ambitions with your manager, so she can help you get the experience you need.

Conclusion

Putting It All Together: Making It Work at Work

The future of work will be created together, not by management or by employees alone.

—*Lee Caraher*

Millennials and Boomer and Gen Xer management are destined to work together for a long time to come, and the companies that figure out how to assimilate Millennial talent positively and cocreate their cultures for the future will have a strategic advantage *as soon as they do it.*

Management need not lie down or bend over backward to accommodate anyone of any age to make this happen. But as managers, we do need to recognize that we need to adjust some practices and policies to harness the energy and potential of all the people around us. We must recognize where our people need to adjust their attitudes, behavior, and understanding to maximize productivity and achieve our business goals. It can be done!

Management, we cannot assume that our younger (or any) colleague knows what is expected from her in terms of work product, behavior, dress, or office hours.

- The more we describe what we expect, the less chance we have of being disappointed.
- Likewise, when our expectations have not been met, do not wait too long before providing helpful, corrective

feedback in a manner that can be heard. Make sure you have been heard.

- Building an appreciative culture will improve your team's performance; find ways to share appreciation for people's efforts and acknowledge good work.
- Find ways to connect with younger colleagues so you have personal insight into how they are feeling and approaching their work. Read what they read; agree to be a mentor; open your door and find time to listen to and talk with your younger team members.

Millennials, if you want a strong say in what the future of work looks like sooner rather than later, you have to carry some of the weight too.

- Pay attention to the people around you in the office. Don't assume that your interpretation of office hours is the same as your manager's. Ask questions before doing things you don't see other people doing.
- Read what your manager reads.
- Take advantage of any training courses that are available.
- Show your older colleagues how to use the apps and devices you use.
- Listen to the feedback given to you. Don't take it personally: assume it's meant to be helpful.
- Bring your ideas on how to do things faster, easier, or better forward by first making sure you understand the outcome you need to generate.

In the end, it's all about people. No one builds a company or career alone. We are all in this together. By bridging the gap between the generations and honoring the strengths we all bring to the table, Millennials and management can cocreate a future-proof business in which people of all ages will flourish.

Notes

Chapter 1

1. Attributed to Socrates by Plato, according to William L. Patty and Louise S. Johnson, *Personality and Adjustment* (New York: McGraw-Hill, 1953), 277.
2. D'Vera Chon "A Demographic Portrait of the Millennial Generation," Pew Research Center, February 24, 2010, http://www.pewsocialtrends.org/2010/02/24/a-demographic-portrait-of-the-millennial-generation/.
3. From the book description for *The Next America,* Paul Taylor and the Pew Research Center (Washington, DC: Public Affairs/Perseus Book Group, 2014)
4. Emily Brandon, "The Ideal Retirement Age," *US News & World Report,* June 10, 2013, http://money.usnews.com/money/retirement/articles/2013/06/10/the-ideal-retirement-age.
5. Carmen DeNavas-Walt et al., "Income, Poverty, and Health Insurance Coverage in the United States: 2012," United States Census Bureau, September 2013, https://www.census.gov/prod/2013pubs/p60-245.pdf.
6. "Women in the Labor Force: A Databook," Bureau of Labor Statistics, February 2013, http://www.bls.gov/cps/wlf-databook-2012.pdf
7. Tim Urban, "Why Generation Y Yuppies Are Unhappy," *The Huffington Post,* September 15, 2013, http://www.huffingtonpost.com/wait-but-why/generation-y-unhappy_b_3930620.html.
8. "2012 HR Beat: A Survey on the Pulse of Today's Global Workforce," SuccessFactors, October 2012, https://www.successfactors.com/en_us/lp/2012-hr-beat.html?Campaign_ID=15722&TAG=Q312_Global_HRBeats_PR&CmpLeadSource=Public%20Relations

Chapter 2

1. Paul Taylor and Scott Keeter, eds., *The Millennial Count,* Pew Research Center, March 22, 2010. http://www.pewsocialtrends.org/2010/02/24/millennials-confident-connected-open-to-change/

2. Derek Thompson, "The Unluckiest Generation: What Will Become of Millennials?" *The Atlantic.com,* April 26, 2013, http://www.theatlantic.com/business/archive/2013/04/the-unluckiest-generation-what-will-become-of-millennials/275336/.

3. "The Cross-Platform Report: A Look Across Screens," The Nielsen Company, June 10, 2013, http://www.nielsen.com/us/en/reports/2013/the-cross-platform-report--a-look-across-screens.html.

4. Paul Taylor and Scott Keeter, eds. *Millennials: A Portrait of Generation Next,* February 2010. http://www.pewsocialtrends.org/files/2010/10/millennials-confident-connected-open-to-change.pdf

5. Andrea Caumont, "6 Key Findings About Going to College," Pew Research Center, February 11, 2014, http://www.pewresearch.org/fact-tank/2014/02/11/6-key-findings-about-going-to-college/.

6. Comments on Barry Salzberg, "What Millennials Want (And Why Employers Should Take Notice)," LinkedIn, January 22, 2014, https://www.linkedin.com/today/post/article/20140122180239-27058877-what-millennials-want-and-why-employers-should-take-notice?trk=vsrp_influencer_content_res_name&trkInfo=V SRPsearchId%3A93841401165051126%2CVSRPtargetId%3A5 831519898698145792%2CVSRPcmpt%3Aprimary.

7. Jolene L. Roehlkepartain, *150 Ways to Show Kids You Care,* Minneapolis, MN: The Search Institute: 2005. http://www.search-institute.org/blog/revised-150-ways-poster

8. Karie Willyerd, "Parents May Be Your Secret Weapon for Recruiting and Retaining Millennials," *HBR Blog Network,* December 23, 2013, http://blogs.hbr.org/2013/12/parents-may-be-your-secret-weapon-for-recruiting-and-retaining-millennials/.

9. Heather L. Messera et al., "D.C.'s New Guard: What Does the Next Generation of American Leaders Think?" The Brookings

Institute, February 2011, http://www.brookings.edu/~/media/ research/files/reports/2011/2/young%20leaders%20singer/02_ young_leaders_singer.pdf.

10. Bruce Drake, "Male Millennials more likely to live at home than females," Pew Research Center, August 14, 2013, http://www .pewresearch.org/fact-tank/2013/08/14/male-millennials-more-likely-to-live-at-home-than-females/.

Chapter 3

1. Jeanne Meister, "Job Hopping Is the 'New Normal' for Millennials," *Forbes.com*, August 14, 2012, http://www.forbes.com/ sites/jeannemeister/2012/08/14/job-hopping-is-the-new-normal-for-millennials-three-ways-to-prevent-a-human-resource-nightmare/.

2. Cliff Zukin and Mark Szeltner, "Talent Report: What Workers Want in 2012 Net Impact," May 2012, Net Impact, https:// netimpact.org/docs/publications-docs/NetImpact_WhatWorkers Want2012.pdf.

Chapter 5

1. Tim Donnelly, "How to Get Feedback from Employees," *Inc.* magazine, August 10, 2010, http://www.inc.com/guides/2010/08/ how-to-get-feedback-from-employees.html.

2. Donnelly, "How to Get Feedback From Employees."

3. Brian Klapper, *The Q-Loop: The Art & Science of Lasting Corporate Change* (Brookline: Bibliomotion, 2013).

Chapter 6

1. Mona Berberich, *BetterWeekDays.com*, 2013. http://blog .betterweekdays.com/blog/employers/326078/how-paying -their-employees-to-quit-earns-zappos-to.

2. For more about the Myers-Briggs Type Indicators, see www .myersbriggs.org.

3. Tom Rath, *Strengths Finders 2.0* (New York: Gallup Press, 2007).

4. For more about the DISC model, see www.thediscpersonalitytest .com.

Chapter 7

1. Stacia Sherman Garr, "The State of Employee Recognition in 2012," Bersin & Associates, June 2012, http://www.achievers .com/webinar/wb-2012-07-19/materials/researchreport-state-of -recognition-2012.pdf.
2. Based on the work of Marcial Losada and Emily Heaphy. "The Role of Positivity and Connectivity in the Performance of Business Teams: A Nonlinear Dynamics Model," *American Behavioral Scientist*, Vol. 47, No. 6 (2004): 740, doi: 10.1177/0002764203260208.
3. "The Suitcase," *Mad Men*, first broadcast September 5, 2010 by AMC, directed by Jennifer Getzinger and written by Matthew Weiner.

Chapter 8

1. Stephen R. Covey, *7 Habits of Highly Effective People* (New York: Simon & Schuster, 1990).
2. Drawn from work of Chris Argyris, cofounder of Organization Development, Professor Emeritus, Harvard Business School, *On Organizational Learning* (New York: Wiley-Blackwell, 1999).
3. Peggy Post and Peter Post, *Emily Post's The Etiquette Advantage in Business* (New York: William Morrow, 2005).

Chapter 9

1. "The Leadership Circle Profile," The Leadership Circle, http:// www.theleadershipcircle.com/assessment-tools/profile.
2. Kim H. Krisco, *Leadership & the Art of Conversation: Conversation as a Management Tool* (Rocklin, CA: Prima Publishing, 1997).
3. Krisco, *Leadership & the Art of Conversation*.
4. Bill Gross, "How to give GREAT employee feedback" LinkedIn, November 30, 2012, http://www.linkedin.com/today/post/ article/20121130041419-9947747-how-to-give-great-employee-feedback.

Chapter 10

1. John Case, *The Open-Book Experience: Lessons from 100 Companies Who Successfully Transformed Themselves* (New York: Basic Books, 1998); *Open-Book Management: The Coming Business Revolution*, (New York: HarperBusiness, 1996).
2. Leerom Segal, et al., *The Decoded Company: Know Your Talent Better Than You Know Your Customers* (New York: Portfolio Hardcover, 2014). Quoted by Alison Griswold, "At Whole Foods, Employees Can Look Up Other Employees' Salaries," *Entreprenuer.com*, March 4, 2014, http://www.entrepreneur.com/article/231940#.

Chapter 11

1. Joan C. Williams, "Meet the New Face of Diversity: The 'Slacker' Millennial Guy," *HBR Blog Network*, October 14, 2013, http://blogs.hbr.org/2013/10/meet-the-new-face-of-diversity-the-slacker-millennial-guy/.
2. Boris Gryosberg and Robin Abrahams, "Manage Your Work, Manage Your Life," *Harvard Business Review*, March 2014, http://hbr.org/2014/03/manage-your-work-manage-your-life/ar/1.
3. Jessica Grose, "Male Executives Don't Feel Guilt, See Work–life Balance As a Women's Problem," *Slate.com*, March 5, 2014, http://www.slate.com/blogs/xx_factor/2014/03/05/harvard_business_review_study_on_work_life_balance_male_executives_see_family.html.
4. Micheline Maynard, "Yahoo's New Policy Exposes the Great WAH Workplace Divide," *Forbes.com,* February 27, 2013, http://www.forbes.com/sites/michelinemaynard/2013/02/27/yahoos-new-policy-exposes-the-great-wah-divide/.

Chapter 12

1. Daniel Goleman, Richard Boyatzis, and Annie McKee, *Primal Leadership: Unleashing the Power of Emotional Intelligence,* 10th anniversary edition (Boston: Harvard Review Press, 2013, xiii.

2. "Affordable Care Act 101," US Small Business Administration, July 2013, page 18, http://www.sba.gov/sites/default/files/files/SBA%20ACA%20101%20Deck%20-%20Updated%20July%202013%20(Disclaimer).pdf.

Chapter 13

1. "2012 HR Beat: A Survey on the Pulse of Today's Global Workforce," Dimensional Research Report, commissioned and published by SuccessFactors, an SAP Company, October 2012, http://www.successfactors.com/en_us/lp/2012-hr-beat.html.
2. Jacquelyn Smith, "How To Be A Great Mentor," *Forbes.com*, May 17, 2013, quoting Pamela Ryckman, *Stiletto Network: Inside the Women's Power Circles That Are Changing the Face of Business* (AMACOM (May 16, 2013) http://www.forbes.com/sites/jacquelynsmith/2013/05/17/how-to-become-a-great-mentor/.
3. Dave Clutterbuck, "Why Mentorships Fail," *Workinfo.com*, December 2002, http://www.workinfo.com/free/downloads/100.htm.
4. Smith, "How To Be A Great Mentor."
5. Karie Willyerd, "Engage a Mentor with a Short-Term Project," *HBR Blog Network*, February 21, 2014, http://blogs.hbr.org/2014/02/engage-a-mentor-with-a-short-term-project/.
6. Mary Dean Sorcinelli and Jung H.Yun, "Office of Faculty Development Mutual Mentoring Guide," UMass Amherst, 2009, http://www.umass.edu/ctfd/mentoring/downloads/Mutual%20Mentoring%20Guide%20Final%2011_20.pdf.

Chapter 14

1. Walt Whitman, "O Captain! My Captain!" 1865.
2. *Dead Poet's Society,* directed by Peter Weir (Touchstone Pictures, 1989).
3. Adam, comment on Urban, "Why Gen Y Yuppies Are Unhappy," http://www.huffingtonpost.com/wait-but-why/generation-y-unhappy_b_3930620.html.
4. Jeanne Meister, "Job Hoping Is the 'New Normal' for Millennials," *Forbes.com*, August 14, 2012.

References

People

Lori Ogden Moore, Executive Coach, OM Associates, San Francisco
Peter Caraher, Social Worker, Millbrae, CA—husband
Abby Uecker, Social Worker, San Mateo, CA—friend, job-share
with Peter Caraher

Sources

"2012 HR Beat: A Survey on the Pulse of Today's Global Workforce." SuccessFactors and Dimensional Research, October 2012. http://www.successfactors.com/en_us/lp/2012-hr-beat.html.

Agan, Tom. "Embracing the Millennials' Mind-Set at Work," *The New York Times*, November 9, 2013. http://www.nytimes.com/2013/11/10/jobs/embracing-the-millennials-mind-set-at-work.html?_r=0.

Berberich, Mona, BetterWeekDays.com, 2013. <<au: Please provide specific article or url>>

Blotter, Jessica. "10 Ways Today's Purpose-Driven Brands Can Bring Their Core Values To Life," *Fastcompany.com*, October 14, 2013. http://www.fastcoexist.com/3019856/10-ways-todays-purpose-driven-brands-can-bring-their-core-values-to-life.

Blue Sky Coaching. "10 Ways to be a Good Mentor." 2008. http://www.blueskycoaching.com.au/pdf/v4i10_mentor.pdf "

Boushey, Heather, and Sarah Jane Glynn. "There Are Significant Business Costs to Replacing Employees." Center for American Progress, November 16, 2012. http://americanprogress.org/issues/labor/report/2012/11/16/44464/there-are-significant-business-costs-to-replacing-employees/.

Brack, Jessica. "Maximizing Millennials in the Workplace." University of North Carolina Kenan-Flagler Business School, 2012. http://www.kenan-flagler.unc.edu/executive-development/custom-

programs/~/media/DF1C11C056874DDA8097271A1ED48662.
ashx.

Brandon, Emily. "The Idea Retirement Age." *US News & World Report*, June 10, 2013. http://money.usnews.com/money/retirement/articles/2013/06/10/the-ideal-retirement-age.

Cadogan, Tim. "10 Lessons in Defining Your Company Values." LinkedIn, May 3, 2013. http://www.linkedin.com/today/post/article/20130503131505-3257535-10-lessons-in-defining-your-company-values.

Capperella, Joe. "Why Millennials Are Immature, Entitled and the Best Hire," *Entrepreneur.com*, December 27, 2013. http://www.entrepreneur.com/article/230536.

Case, John. *Open-Book Management: The Coming Business Revolution*. New York: HarperBusiness, 1996.

Caumont, Andrea. "6 key findings about going to college." Pew Research Center, February 11, 2014. http://www.pewresearch.org/fact-tank/2014/02/11/6-key-findings-about-going-to-college/.

Chon, D'Vera. "A Demographic Portrait of the Millennial Generation." Pew Research Center, February 24 2010. http:// pewsocialtrends.org/2010/02/24/a-demographic-portrait-of-the-millennial-generation/.

Clutterbuck, Dave. "Why Mentorships Fail." Workinfo.com, 2002. http://workinfo.com/free/downloads/100.htm.

Covey, Stephen R. *7 Habits of Highly Effective People: Powerful Lessons in Personal Change*. New York: Simon & Schuster, 1990.

Dead Poet's Society. DVD. Directed by Peter Weir. 1989; Anaheim, CA: Touchstone Home Entertainment, 1998.

Dearborn, Jenny. "Eight Tactics to Increase Millennial Productivity in the Workplace." SAP Business Trends, September 18, 2013. http://scn.sap.com/community/business-trends/blog/2013/09/18/eight-tactics-to-increase-millennial-productivity-in-the-workplace.

DeNavas-Walt, Carmen, Bernadette D. Proctor, and Jessica C. Smith. "Income, Poverty, and Health Insurance Coverage in the United States: 2012." United States Census Bureau, September 2013. https://www.census.gov/prod/2013pubs/p60-245.pdf. Donnelly, Tim, "How to Get Feedback From Employees," *Inc.com*, inc.com/guides/2010/08/how-to-get-feedback-from-employees.html.

Drake, Bruce, "Male Millennials more likely to live at home than females." The Pew Research Center, August 14, 2013. http://pewresearch.org/fact-tank/2013/08/14/male-millennials-more-likely-to-live-at-home-than-females/.

Freeman, Elissa. "Learning to Love Working With Millennials," *Entrepreneur.com*, September 3, 2013. http://www.entrepreneur.com/article/228161.

Fry, Richard. "A Rising Share of Young Adults Live in Their Parent's Home." Pew Research Center, August 1, 2013. http://www.pewsocialtrends.org/2013/08/01/a-rising-share-of-young-adults-live-in-their-parents-home/.

Fry, Richard. "Young Adults after the Recession: Fewer Homes, Fewer Cars, Less Debt." Pew Research Center, February 21, 2013. http://www.pewsocialtrends.org/2013/02/21/young-adults-after-the-recession-fewer-homes-fewer-cars-less-debt/.

Galinsky, Ellen, Kimberlee Salmond, James T. Bond, Marcia Brumit Kropf, Meredith Moore, and Brad Harrington. "Leaders in a Global Economy: A Study of Executive Women and Men." Families and Work Institute, Catalyst, and the Center for Work & Family at Boston College Carroll School of Management, January 2003. http://www.bc.edu/content/dam/files/centers/cwf/research/publications/pdf/BC-FWI_Global_Leaders_Full_Study.pdf.

Garr, Stacia. "The State of Employee Recognition in 2012." Bersin & Associates, June 2012. http://marketing.bersin.com/Recognition.html <<au: hyperlink is broken>>

Goleman, Daniel, Richard Boyatzis, and Annie McKee. *Primal Leadership: Unleashing the Power of Emotional Intelligence*, 10th anniversary edition. Boston: Harvard Review Business Press, 2013.

Green, Sarah, and Walter Frick. "Millennial Women Aren't Opting Out; They're Doubling Down." *HBR Blog Network*, August 8, 2013. http://blogs.hbr.org/2013/08/millennial-women-arent-opting/.

Griswold, Alison. "At Whole Foods, Employees Can Look Up Other Employees' Salaries." *Entrepreneur.com*, March 4, 2014. http://entrepreneur.com/article/231940#.

Grose, Jessica. "Male Executives Don't Feel Guilt, See Work–life Balance As a Women's Problem." *Slate.com*, March 5, 2014. http://slate.com/blogs/xx_factor/2014/03/05/harvard_

business_review_study_on_work_life_balance_male_executives_
see_family.html.

Gross, Bill. "How to give GREAT employee feedback." LinkedIn, November 30, 2012. http://www.linkedin.com/today/post/article/ 20121130041419-9947747-how-to-give-great-employee-feedback.

Gryosberg, Boris, and Robin Abrahams. "Manage Your Work, Manage Your Life." *Harvard Business Review*, March 2014. http:// hbr.org/2014/03/manage-your-work-manage-your-life/ar/1.

Harper, Mitch. "Want To Hire Superstars? 7 Questions To Ask During Interviews." *Wired*, June 28, 2013. http://insights.wired .com/profiles/blogs/want-to-hire-superstars-here-are-7-questions-to-ask-during#axzz33nhh75oc.

Holland, Kelley. "Millennials Managers Seen as 'Entitled'," *Entrepreneur.com*, September 4, 2013. http://www.entrepreneur.com/ article/228191.

Howells, Richard. "When It Comes To Changing The World, Millennials Mean Business." *Forbes.com*, September 25, 2013. http://www.forbes.com/sites/sap/2013/09/25/when-it-comes-to-changing-the-world-millennials-mean-business/.

Huspeni, Andrea. "Millennials Are Snubbing the Corporate World for Entrepreneurship," *Entrepreneur.com,* September 23, 2013. http://www.entrepreneur.com/article/228464.

John Case, John. *The Open-Book Experience: Lessons from 100 Companies Who Successfully Transformed Themselves*. New York: Basic Books, 1998.

Kaplan, Janice. "Gratitude Survey." John Templeton Foundation, June-October 2012. http://greatergood.berkeley.edu/images/ uploads/JTF_GRATITUDE_REPORTpub.doc.

Klapper, Brian. *The Q-Loop: The Art & Science of Lasting Corporate Change*. Brookline: Bibliomotion, 2013.

Knight, Matt. "Biz leaders should focus on people not target, says report." *CNN.com*, January 22, 2010. http://www.cnn .com/2010/BUSINESS/01/19/leadership.people.focus.report/.

Krisco, Kim H. *Leadership & the Art of Conversation: Conversation as a Management Tool*. Rocklin, CA: Prima Publishing, 1997.

Larson, Gloria, and Mike Metzger. "Why Everyone is Wrong About Working With Millennials." *Fast Company*, December 3, 2013.

http://fastcompany.com/3022520/why-everyone-is-wrong-about-working-with-millennials.

Losada, Marcial, and Emily Heaphy. "The Role of Positivity and Connectivity in the Performance of Business Teams: A Nonlinear Dynamics Model," *American Behavioral Scientist*, Vol. 47, No. 6 (2004): 740. doi: 10.1177/0002764203260208.

Max, D.T. "Happiness 101." The *New York Times*, January 7, 2007. http://www.nytimes.com/2007/01/07/magazine/07happin css.t.html?pagewanted=all.

Maynard, Micheline. "Yahoo's New Policy Exposes the Great WAH Workplace Divide." *Forbes.com*, February 27, 2013. http://forbes.com/sites/michelinemaynard/2013/02/27/yahoos-new-policy-exposes-the-great-wah-divide/.

McDonald, Kadi. "How to navigate the Millennial candidate pool." Third Sector Today, January 28, 2014. http://thirdsectortoday. com/2014/01/28/how-to-navigate-the-millennial-candidate-pool/.

Meister, Jeanne. "Job Hopping Is the 'New Normal' for Millennials: Three Ways to Prevent a Human Resource Nightmare." *Forbes .com*, August 14, 2012. http://www.forbes.com/sites/jeannemeis ter/2012/08/14/job-hopping-is-the-new-normal-for-millennials-three-ways-to-prevent-a-human-resource-nightmare/

Monica, "25 Staff Appreciation and Recognition Ideas that Won't Break the Bank," *People Metrics,* July 31, 2009 **<<au: please provide a URL>>**

National Business Research Institute. "Soliciting Employee Feedback: Getting Results." http://www.nbrii.com/employee-survey-white-papers/soliciting-employee-feedback-getting-results/

Parker, Kim. "The Boomerang Generation." Pew Research Center, March 15, 2012. http://www.pewsocialtrends.org/2012/03/15/the-boomerang-generation/.

Patty, William L., and Louise S. Johnson. *Personality and Adjustment.* New York: McGraw-Hill, 1953.

Pew Research Center. "Millennials: Confident. Connected. Open to Change." February 2010. http://pewsocialtrends.org/files/2010/10/millennials-confident-connected-open-to-change.pdf.

Pew Research Center. "On Pay Gap, Millennial Women Near Parity—For Now." December 11, 2013. http://www.pewsocialtrends.org /2013/12/11/on-pay-gap-millennial-women-near-parity-for-now/.

Post, Peggy and Peter Post. *Emily Post's The Etiquette Advantage in Business: Personal Skills for Professional Success*. New York: William Morrow, 2005.

Pozin, Ilya. "How Transparent Is Too Transparent In Business?" *Forbes.com*, April 2, 2014. http://forbes.com/sites/ilyapozin/2014/04/02/how-transparent-is-too-transparent/

Rath, Tom. *StrengthsFinders 2.0*. New York: Gallup Press, 2007.

Rikleen, Lauren Stiller. "Where they're coming from." *Communication World*, February 2014, Vol. 31 Issue 2.

Roehlkepartain, Jolene L. *150 Ways to Show Kids You Care*. Minneapolis, MN: The Search Institute, 2005. [Au: author? is it a paper? a book? an article? URL available?]

Salzberg, Barry, "What Millennials Want (And Why Employers Should Take Notice)," LinkedIn, January 22, 2014. http://linkedin.com/today/post/article/20140122180239-27058877-what-millennials-want-and-why-employers-should-take-notice?trk=vsrp_influencer_content_res_name&trkInfo=VSRPsearchId%3A93841401165051126%2CVSRPtargetId%3A5831519898698145792%2CVSRPcmpt%3Aprimary

Schawbel, Dan. "Multi-Generational Worker Attitudes." Monster.com and Millennial Branding. March 14, 2013. http://www.about-monster.com/sites/default/files/MillennialBrandingMulti-GenerationalWorkerAttitudesWhitePaper.pdf.

Schultz, Rachael. "5 Things Every New Boss Should Know." *Men's Health*, November 26, 2013. http://www.menshealth.com/best-life/new-boss-lessons.

Segal, Leerom, Aaron Goldstein, Jay Goldman, and Rahaf Harfoush. *The Decoded Company: Know Your Talent Better Than You Know Your Customers*. New York: Portfolio Hardcover, 2014.

Singer, P.W., Heather Messera, and Brendan Orino. "D.C.'s New Guard: What Does the Next Generation of American Leaders Think?" The Brookings Institute, February 2011. http://www.brookings.edu/~/media/research/files/reports/2011/2/young%20leaders%20singer/02_young_leaders_singer.pdf.

Singer, Peter. "Millennial Generation the Next Big Thing," *CNN.com*, March 24, 2011. http://www.cnn.com/2011/OPINION/03/24/singer.young.leaders/.

Smith, Jacquelyn. "How To Be A Great Mentor." *Forbes.com,* May 17, 2013, quoting Pamela Ryckman, *Stiletto Network: Inside the Women's Power Circles That Are Changing the Face of Business,* New York: AMACOM, May 16, 2013) [**Au: the title is a book, published by AMACOM, so what is the Forbes cite? is it from a book review? Info needs to be clarified**]

Society for Human Resource Management, the. "2012 Employee Job Satisfaction and Engagement: How Employees Are Dealing With Uncertainty." 2012. http://www.shrm.org/Research/SurveyFindings/Articles/Documents/SHRM-Employee-Job-Satisfaction-Engagement.pdf.

Society for Human Resource Management for Globoforce, the. "Fall 2012 Report: The Business Impact of Employee Recognition." Fall 2012. http://go.globoforce.com/rs/globoforce/images/SHRMFALL2012Survey_web.pdf.

Sorcinelli, Mary Dean, and Jung H. Yun. "Office of Faculty Development Mutual Mentoring Guide." UMass Amherst, 2009. http://umass.edu/ctfd/mentoring/downloads/Mutual%20Mentoring%20Guide%20Final%2011_20.pdf.

Stephans, John. "How Corporate America Overcame Its Fear of Millennials," *Wired.com,* January 13, 2014. http://www.wired.com/2014/01/corporate-america-overcame-fear-millennials/.

Stillman, Jessica. "Does Gen Y depend too much on parents for career advice?" *Brazen Careerist,* November 13, 2012. http://blog.brazencareerist.com/2012/11/13/does-gen-y-depend-too-much-on-parents-for-career-advice/.

Keeter, Scott, and Paul Taylor. "The Millennials." Pew Research Center, December 9, 2009. http://www.pewresearch.org/2009/12/10/the-millennials/.

Taylor, Paul, and the Pew Research Center. *The Next America: .Boomers, Millennials, and the Looming Generational Showdown.* Washington, D.C.: PublicAffairs, 2014.

"The Cross-Platform Report: A Look Across Screens." The Nielsen Company, June 10, 2013. http://www.nielsen.com/us/en/reports/2013/the-cross-platform-report--a-look-across-screens.html.

"The Leadership Circle Profile." The Leadership Circle. http://www.theleadershipcircle.com/assessment-tools/profile.

"The Suitcase," Mad Men. First broadcast September 5, 2010 by AMC. Directed by Jennifer Getzinger and written by Matthew Weiner.

Thompson, Derek. "Adulthood, Delayed: What Has the Recession Done to Millennials?" *The Atlantic*, February 14, 2012. http://www.theatlantic.com/business/archive/2012/02/adulthood-delayed-what-has-the-recession-done-to-millennials/252913/.

Thompson, Derek. "The Unluckiest Generation: What Will Become of Millennials?" *The Atlantic*, April 26, 2013. http://www.theatlantic.com/business/archive/2013/04/the-unluckiest-generation-what-will-become-of-millennials/275336/.

Urban, Tim. "Why Generation Y Yuppies Are Unhappy." The Huffington Post, September 15, 2013. http://www.huffingtonpost.com/wait-but-why/generation-y-unhappy_b_3930620.html.

US Small Business Administration. "Affordable Care Act 101: What The Health Care Law Means for Small Businesses." July 2013. http://sba.gov/sites/default/files/files/SBA%20ACA%20101%20Deck%20-%20Updated%20July%202013%20(Disclaimer).pdf.

Von Bank, Hannah. "On the Job: 4 Insights for Engaging the Millennial Generation," *Allen Interactions*, February 4, 2014. http://info.alleninteractions.com/bid/101204/On-the-Job-4-Insights-for-Engaging-the-Millennial-Generation.

Weinstein, Adam. "I'm Gen Y, and I'm Not a Special Snowflake. I'm Broke." *MotherJones.com*, September 20, 2013. http://www.motherjones.com/politics/2013/09/generation-y-millennials-entitled-poor.

Williams, Joan C. "Meet the New Face of Diversity: The 'Slacker' Millennial Guy." *HBR Blog Network*, October 14, 2013. http://blogs.hbr.org/2013/10/meet-the-new-face-of-diversity-the-slacker-millennial-guy/.

Willyerd, Karie. "Engage a Mentor with a Short-Term Project." *HBR Blog Network*, February 21, 2014. http://blogs.hbr.org/2014/02/engage-a-mentor-with-a-short-term-project/

Willyerd, Karie. "Parents May Be Your Secret Weapon For Recruiting and Retaining Millennials." *HBR Blog Network*, December 23, 2013. http://blogs.hbr.org/2013/12/parents-may-be-your-secret-weapon-for-recruiting-and-retaining-millennials/.

Winograd, Morley, and Michael Hais. "How Millennials Could Upend Wall Street and Corporate America." The Brooking Institute,

May 2014. http://www.brookings.edu/research/papers/2014/05/ millenials-upend-wall-street-corporate-america-winograd-hais.

"Women in the Labor Force: A Databook." Bureau of Labor Statistics, February 2013. http://www.bls.gov/cps/wlf-databook-2012 .pdf.

Young Entrepreneur Council. "10 Ways to get honest feedback from your employees." *SmartBlog on Leadership*, May 8, 2013. http:// smartblogs.com/leadership/2013/05/08/10-ways-to-get-honest-feedback-from-your-employees/.

Zengler, Jack, and Joseph Folkman. "Your Employees Want the Negative Feedback You Hate to Give." *HBR Blog Network*, January 15, 2014. http://blogs.hbr.org/2014/01/your-employees-want-the-negative-feedback-you-hate-to-give/.

Zukin, Cliff, and Mark Szeltner. "Talent Report: What Workers Want in 2012." Net Impact, May 2012. https://netimpact.org/ docs/publications-docs/NetImpact_WhatWorkersWant2012 .pdf.

Index

directions, 112
for interview, 73

E
economy, Millennials challenge in
finding jobs, 25–26
education
grade inflation, 17–18
quality of, 16–18
e-mail
dos and don'ts, 106
etiquette, 113–114
providing directions through,
103–106
thanks in, 83–84, 87
embarrassing feedback, 129
emoticons, 85
employee education and training, 157
employee first method, 156
employee match program, 52
employee roles, value of position,
47–48
enablers, 21–22
encouragers, 21–22
enthusiasm, 56
etiquette, e-mail, 113–114
expectations, reinforcing
through games, 114–115
through reference guides, 115
through staff reminders, 115–116
extroverts and introverts, 68–69

F
Facebook, access to leadership, 157
facts, conflict communication
wheel, 127
feedback
communication circle, 126–127
conflict communication wheel,
126–128
conflict resolution, 125–126
and criticism, 124

effective language for, 122–124
embarrassing, 129
generous, 128
management dos and don'ts,
129–130
milestone setting, 125
Millennial dos and don'ts, 130
and Millennial mindset, 33–34
need and desire for, 119, 121–122
power of "and," 123–124
soliciting input, 60–62
through surveys, 61–62
timing of, 120
tough conversations, 125–128
feelings, conflict communication
wheel, 127
first time job interviews, 71
flexible schedules. *See also*
work-life balance
advantages, 136, 138–139
attitude toward, 140–143
Baby Boomer mindset, 144
common courtesy, 144–145
divide in perception, 139
guidelines for, 145–148
and high-performance project
work, 138
inconsistencies, 138
management dos and don'ts,
148–149
Millennial dos and don'ts, 149
and Millennial mindset,
136–137
retracted schedules, 135–136
taking for granted, 144
technology and remote work,
137–146
formed ideas, soliciting input, 62
freedom, and Millennial mindset,
34–35
full-life balance. *See* flexible
schedules; work-life balance

Acknowledgments

First and foremost, thank you to the employees of Double Forte who have lived through us figuring this out! Your steadfast belief and confidence in me is humbling—I appreciate your willingness to try new things even when you thought I was off the wall. That you are part of the team is truly my proudest career achievement. Thank you especially to my colleague and fellow author Liz O, who not only encouraged me to share what we've learned, but introduced me to Bibliomotion. And of course to Stephanie and Czar, who got this whole ball rolling.

Thank you to the hundreds of people who either spent time with me, my e-mails, or my surveys—your input and ideas have been invaluable.

Many thanks to Jill, Erika, Jill, Shevaun, and all of the staff, authors, and friends of Bibliomotion; it's an incredible community I'm honored to be a part of.

And love and so much appreciation for Pete, Michael and Liam, my biggest fans—you are why I do what I do.

About the Author

Lee McEnany Caraher is the founder and CEO of Double Forte, a fiercely independent marketing firm doing great work for good people and companies. She is also the founder of Rocks Are Hard, a colorful blog delivering advice, strong opinion, and research on leadership and management of people of all ages, MBTI types, DISC profiles, strengths, and growing edges. Lee graduated from Carleton College with a bachelor of arts in history—well Medieval History, which she finds useful every day. She lives near San Francisco, with her husband, two children, and a blind cat, and serves on the board of directors of several prominent San Francisco Bay Area nonprofit organizations.